Tailored Learning:

Designing the Blend That Fits

JENNIFER HOFMANN AND NANETTE MINER

Alexandria, Virginia

ASTD Press is an internationally renowned source of insightful and practical information on workplace learning and performance topics, including training basics, evaluation and return-on-investment, instructional systems development, e-learning, leadership, and career development.

Ordering information: Books published by ASTD Press can be purchased by visiting our website at store.astd.org or by calling 800.628.2783 or 703.683.8100.

Library of Congress Control Number: 2008932276

ISBN-10: 1-56286-551-X
ISBN-13: 978-1-56286-551-1

ASTD Press Editorial Staff:

Director: Dean Smith
Manager, Acquisitions and Author Relations: Mark Morrow
Editorial Manager: Jacqueline Edlund-Braun
Senior Associate Editor: Tora Estep
Editorial Assistant: Georgina Del Priore

Copyeditor: Ann Bruen
Indexer: April Davis
Proofreader: Kris Patenaude
Interior Design and Production: PerfecType, Nashville, TN
Cover Design: Steve Fife
Cover Illustration: flashfilm

Printed by Versa Press, Inc. East Peoria, Illinois; www.versapress.com

Contents

Preface

Before the advent of broadband wireless access, streaming media, and many other now-familiar technologies, the word *training* meant the same thing to nearly everyone. Training conjured up visions of flipcharts; marker boards; tables set up in rows; participant guides; textbooks; completion certificates; and often, day after day of classes in distant hotel conference rooms. *Tailored Learning: Designing the Blend That Fits* addresses today's completely changed training realities in a unique way.

Throughout this book, you will be offered a "fly-on-the-wall" perspective of a training consultancy (of which you are a valuable member) that has been tasked with redesigning a traditional, classroom-based new hire sales training program and presenting multiple options to a fictitious client for more effective delivery that achieves the goals of the program.

Our approach is a structured methodology that assesses the ability of various delivery methods (classroom, synchronous, and asynchronous) to support the learning objectives of the new hire training curriculum. The approach begins with the redesign of the existing face-to-face classroom program, which is done for the following reasons:

- to ensure that the client can understand the assessment of the objectives of the existing course in a way that makes sense to him or her
- to ensure that we can achieve the learning goals in a traditional, two-day training event in case the client believes the blended approach is too complex or, for organizational reasons, it cannot be achieved (lack of access to technology, monetary constraints).

Once the classroom approach is redesigned, we begin to analyze the use of more technological training solutions to achieve the same learning outcomes. At each phase of our redesign, we ask pertinent questions, such as "Will the learner be successful with this approach? How can the organization support this delivery methodology? Is an instructor necessary to make this piece of content successful?" The process culminates in the selection of the best blended delivery approach, based on organizational constraints, learner abilities, management support, and the timeline necessary to achieve learner success.

The book is not intended to be read from cover to cover; however, we do recommend reading chapters 1 through 3, so that you will understand the training curriculum that is the basis of the book and the importance of identifying and clarifying achievable learning objectives. Once you have read these chapters, you may choose to read the chapters that follow in any order, depending on your interest: a better classroom design, a blended solution, or alternative training technologies? Chapters 4, 5, 6, and 7 provide you with a carefully detailed design plan for the new hire training curriculum in a given delivery modality. We hope this structured, analytical process will help readers and potential designers of blended learning curriculums to see the design process in a new light where the focus is on performance objectives and organizational needs, rather than on available delivery technology.

Chapter 1

Setting the Stage for the Blend That Fits

The learning approach taken by this book is unique. By building on a common training offering—new hire sales training for the fictional ABC Company—readers get a "fly-on-the-wall" experience as the existing classroom training program is analyzed, dissected, and then reassembled in various formats: classroom; asynchronous; synchronous; and, finally, the culmination of the best of each—a blended offering.

However, before introducing the new hire sales training program, this chapter will provide background and the reasoning behind why the learning approach offered in this book will enable you to produce effective learning programs. The chapter will help you

- understand the evolving learning environment
- make initial decisions about blending learning choices
- prepare your organization to implement a blended solution
- use the book effectively.

THE CHANGING WORLD OF TRAINING

Thirty years ago, *training* meant the same thing to just about everyone: a traditional classroom, complete with flipcharts, marker boards, and tables set up in a particular arrangement. Participant guides, textbooks, and completion certificates were the expected artifacts. Programs were replete with objectives, agendas, and role-play activities. Participants traveled to wherever the instructor was—whether in a different building or different city—and at the end of the experience they were "trained." Training events ranged from a full day of training to five-day intensive "boot camps." No matter the program's overall length, the format always centered on a full day of attendance and participation. Programs proved effective when they required active participation; less effective programs simply required participants to show up.

Today, organizations have vastly different training needs. New hires no longer start jobs or training at the same time. Transporting instructors and participants to one location to attend training classes is not economical and often is disruptive to business and familial commitments. Training needs are frequently immediate; organizations rarely have the luxury of waiting until the next class is scheduled or "enough" people are ready to be trained. Unfortunately, traditional training models often cannot accommodate today's business needs.

The Evolving Field of Training Delivery

Over the past several decades, a number of factors have changed the thinking behind the way training should be delivered. Coinciding with the explosion of technologies available for individual use (via desktop computers; the Internet; and, most recently, various forms of personal digital assistants or PDAs) was the emergence of a global economy, where clients, suppliers, and employees could be located in nearly any part of the world, speak any language, and reside in any time zone. The pace of change severely affected individuals and organizations alike, which in turn changed the way training was delivered and received.

New training technologies and tools were developed to meet this need. Unfortunately, training departments did not really know how to use them, and the resulting misuse (or sometimes overuse) resulted in less than optimal results. With the abundance and proliferation of these new training technologies, proper instructional design methods seemed to become less and less important.

Perhaps the most familiar example of the misuse of a training technology is the "death by PowerPoint" phenomenon, which occurs when the ubiquitous Microsoft presentation (emphasis on the word *presentation*) program is used to deliver boring, information-only "training" sessions. A simple tool that was supposed to be an aid to training actually *became* the training. Standards became lax—if content could be condensed to six bullet points of six words each, it often was labeled as "training." Instructors and instructional designers seemed to become less necessary—after all, why couldn't the same subject matter experts (SMEs) with the content in their heads simply type what they knew onto slides and then lecture?

This is not a criticism of PowerPoint. The question to ask is, "What did instructors do *before* they had easy access to this tool?" They applied sound instructional design principles that ensured the transfer of training. With the advent (and overuse) of technology, "training" degraded to "knowledge sharing."

The problems with training delivery did not stop with our culture's addiction to PowerPoint. The industry added more tools to the mix—CD-ROMs, web-based tutorials, Flash movies, online assessments, virtual classrooms—not to mention the wave of web 2.0 technologies like wikis, blogs, collaborative communities, and virtual worlds. Most were hailed as relatively easy for a "non-technical" person to use. Excitement about them was generated through the use of high-end demonstrations and product launches, which were notably *not* created by "non-technical" folks. This situation led to the assumption that anyone could develop effective instruction using these technologies.

Each new technology had (and continues to have) a great deal of instructional potential, but adoption was burdened by several implementation issues: It seemed so easy to create training using these technologies that instructional design was put aside for the belief that SMEs could channel their expertise through technology and, as if by magic, create training. The common result, no matter what technology was implemented, was a plethora of *information* without collaboration, interactivity, and kinesthetic design. By eliminating opportunities to interact and collaborate, we had eliminated practice, minimized assimilation opportunities, and (basically) crossed our fingers and hoped that some level of mastery was achieved. The result was training designed by SMEs and delivered via some kind of technology, which generally did not meet the same level of effectiveness as traditional classroom instruction.

The choice of delivery medium became more important than the content. The chosen development tool often dictated what was included in the course design. If the tool did not include a quizzing component, then no quizzes were included in the instruction. If a tool included "cool" animations, then animations were included whether or not they had instructional value.

The more complex technologies—Authorware, Toolbook, Flash, and video, to name a few—required programming expertise and a comparatively large budget to produce. Again, the classroom design approach was sidelined and training design fell into the lap of computer programmers. The common result was content that was visually stimulating and exciting, but not instructionally sound.

The Devolving World of Training Design

We have now (d)evolved to the point where SMEs have access to an arsenal of training technologies, and training experts know how to design effective learning solutions. A misguided perception exists that the use of technology has eliminated the need for a designer. Organizations often select a delivery tool because of expediency. Either "this is the tool we already have" or "this is the only way we can create something in the next two weeks." But having a tool does not give you ability. That is akin to saying, "If you own a typewriter you can write the great American novel." Subject matter expertise or programming ability does not equate to the development of effective training programs. Often delivery methodologies are rejected outright because trainers assume that certain topics have to be delivered in certain ways (for example, "You can only teach leadership in the classroom"). When training does not meet the mark, most of the deficiencies are the result of the lack of solid instructional design. This can occur for a number of reasons:

- Professionals are being thrown into roles for which they are not prepared.
- SMEs are becoming trainers.
- Trainers are expected to be able to create electronic media.
- Instructional designers are dismissed because it takes "too much time to go through the design process."

This has left us with a lot of technology and information—but not much actual *training*. With so many professionals and training options at our disposal, it is now time to choose from the best that each has to offer and begin to create training that again hits its instructional mark and provides value to both the individual trainee and the organization.

WHY BLENDED LEARNING?

In the *ASTD E-Learning Handbook* (Rossett, 2002, p. A1), Elliot Masie argues that "we are, as a species, blended learners." Masie is implying that we never, unless forced, learn in a vacuum. If we read a textbook and have a question, we ask a peer or an instructor. If we are listening to a lecture, we take notes and review later. In the modern information age, many of us are apt to use our mobile devices when we want to get more information about something. In short, we combine resources until we have discovered what we need to learn (see the sidebar "Training Methodologies").

Training Methodologies

Classroom	We are all familiar with classroom-based learning from our years of grade school. Typically eight to 25 people attend a training session at one time. The course is led by a facilitator or team of facilitators who follow an agenda. Classroom-based courses last from two hours to 10 weeks depending on the content being taught.
E-Learning: CBT	CBT refers to computer-based training. Before the emergence of the Internet, it was common to distribute training via CD-ROM or to have trainees access a computer-based course from a stand-alone machine. The Video Professor (www.videoprofessor .com) is a great example of CBT.
E-Learning: WBT	Similar to CBT, WBT (web-based training) became popular once the Internet was utilized as a business tool. WBT courses are accessed via the Internet and either downloaded or executed directly from the website. WBT courses can be commercially available (such as the tutorials available from http://office .microsoft.com) or may be proprietary and hosted on an organization's intranet—allowing access to only its employees.
E-Learning: Asynchronous	Asynchronous learning is completed independently and at one's own pace; it is not constrained by geography or time. CBT and WBT courses are both asynchronous training methodologies because the trainee can access them at a time that is convenient for him or her, can review them again and again, and can leave and return to the program as necessary. The learning is not dependent on a time, a place, other learners, or an instructor.
E-Learning: Synchronous	Synchronous learning, by definition, occurs among participants, simultaneously. Classroom-based learning is synchronous learning. E-learning that occurs synchronously requires all participants and a facilitator to simultaneously access an online classroom (such as WebEx, Elluminate, or Centra).

(continued on page 6)

Training Methodologies (continued)

Self-Study	A self-study course is typically paper based, such as a book or training manual. Teaching yourself to use Excel by reading *Excel for Dummies* is an example.
Blended Learning	Blended learning is a combination of training methodologies (see list above), which uses the best delivery method for the successful achievement of the learning objective. For example: Negotiation skills are better taught in a classroom or synchronous environment, which allows for real-time interaction, than in an asynchronous or self-study course. Blended learning means that one course may use three, four, or five methodologies depending on the objectives being taught.

Asynchronous learning, or learning without direct interaction with an instructor, independent of a blend, does not allow us to follow this natural tendency to combine learning types. Typically, if a person is listening to a recorded lecture and has a question, that question goes unanswered. Or, if someone is participating in a self-paced tutorial and gets stuck (either instructionally or technologically), the learning gets placed on the back burner in lieu of something that always is ready and waiting—real work.

This leaves trainees longing for the interaction and support provided by the classroom. Because we've developed a culture that doesn't "allow" us to bring people together for short periods of time (if we bring them together, it's for four or six or eight hours), the classroom experience is often overloaded with an abundance of information (oftentimes more than the trainees really need) and is expensive in terms of time, money, and resources.

In theory, creating a blend solves these problems. Blended learning allows us to exploit the advantages of self-paced learning, while making live interaction, via traditional classroom, synchronous classroom, or even telephone, more valuable, because that time is used almost exclusively for exploration and higher-level learning instead of passing on "information."

In *The Handbook of Blended Learning* (Bonk and Graham, 2006, p. 8), Charles Graham identifies three primary reasons for selecting a blended learning solution:

1. Learning outcomes can be improved over stand-alone delivery methods. By exploiting the advantages of classroom, asynchronous, and synchronous higher learning, value can be achieved.
2. Participants can learn from any location, and there is often flexibility in schedule as well. For example, classroom programs can be great for the

people able to attend and fully commit to longer training interventions, but are limited because they are delivered at a certain time in a certain place, thereby leaving out potential participants because of availability and location. Blended learning can eliminate the need to co-locate participants and instructor, and substantially reduce "live" time commitments, when some learning is accomplished at a time more convenient to the participant.

3. Stand-alone delivery methods can be very costly. A three-day new hire orientation program for a geographically dispersed work group can quickly rack up the costs in terms of travel and related expenses, not to mention the cost of maintaining the classroom. At the other end of the spectrum, a curriculum that is totally asynchronous in nature can be very expensive to build (program) and monitor. By blending classroom, asynchronous, and synchronous components together, as a design might dictate, you can maximize learning by minimizing costs. (See the sidebar "What Does the Term 'Blend' Mean?")

What Does the Term "Blend" Mean?

Not too long ago, a "blend" simply meant doing some pre-work prior to coming to a live event. For example, we worked on a project to create a blended solution for a high-tech firm. The firm wanted to use off-the-shelf leadership development classes, but did not want to send thousands of people to a training site or classroom. In conjunction with the content provider, we devised a blended approach that included these elements:

- Self-study e-learning pre-work, which concluded with a worksheet the individuals needed to print out and bring to the "live" class.
- A virtual class that put participants in breakout rooms to role play and practice various leadership skills. The key here was that individuals had to have completed their pre-work to be able to participate successfully in the classroom portion.
- An on-the-job performance of the skill they had learned and practiced, again using the pre-work sheet, which required them to document how they applied their learning.

The key to making this whole process work was that each piece of the blend was dependent on another. It was obvious, even to the participants, that the asynchronous work and the synchronous work were equally important.

RESURRECTING TRAINING

The next generation of training integrates the best elements of classroom and technologically delivered training. This is where the blend comes into play. Training development professionals, who understand the nature of how people learn, must lead the transformation to *tailored learning* by making the best choice for the curriculum and the audience.

Training professionals now have the freedom to change the paradigm of training as an "event." Not too long ago, a "blend" simply meant doing some pre-work prior to coming to a live event. The blend of the future may include pre-work, classroom, technologically delivered training (synchronous or asynchronous), post-session follow-up or coaching, and a multitude of other delivery mediums. The key is that instructional design methods must be used to create content. This means constructing appropriate objectives, designing exercises and assessments to ensure learning objectives are met, and then selecting the best delivery medium for each individual objective.

When designing a learning blend, the design of the *entire curriculum* is paramount. No individual delivery method is more important than another. Rather, each component *depends* on the others. This requires a new mindset for instructors and audience alike. The most effective learning experience(s) use multiple technologies, selected as the best match for a particular learning objective, eliminating the traditional language of "pre-work," "learning event," and "follow-up." The blended learning environment is based more on trainee success than on instructor control or available technology.

Where to start? An organization needs a solid grasp of the advantages and disadvantages of the various delivery methodologies from an instructional perspective, understanding that a single delivery method will probably not be the optimal solution. That is not as easy as it sounds. For example, it might be "obvious" that a mechanic's course needs to be taught in a hands-on lab environment. And, if an organization had to select a stand-alone delivery method, a lab or an on the-job-approach might be the only option. Once a blend becomes a possibility, however, many more options become available. Perhaps a self-paced tutorial could address workplace safety, and a virtual session could allow trainees to speak with seasoned mechanics about typical repair scenarios. New mechanics would still need to work hands-on in the field, but group instruction could be supplemented by structured mentoring on the job.

IS THE ORGANIZATION READY?

Organizational readiness is *not* a primary goal of this book; however, it should be considered prior to embarking on the creation of a blended curriculum. Sometimes, the way an organization determines its readiness (or lack thereof) is by implementing a blended curriculum and seeing what happens.

An organization should do the following prior to investing time and resources in creating a blended solution:

Create a business case for the investment. Answer the questions: "Why do we want to create a blend? Why is it better than what we are doing now? How will we know the blend works?"

Provide management with reasonable expectations. Often, managers do not know what to expect. Explain that a blended solution does not necessarily preclude travel. Communicate that an online solution will probably require a printed participant workbook. And, ensure up front that employees will be given the time and resources they need to learn independently from their desks. If management does not follow through on supporting the trainees' needs, then the proposition is doomed to failure.

Obtain a sponsor. An initiative of this size will probably bring up hitherto unrecognized issues. A well-placed internal advocate is critical to helping get past any bumps along the way.

CONSIDER YOUR OPTIONS BEFORE YOU DECIDE

Just because the organization is (potentially) ready for a blended learning solution does not mean that it is the correct approach. It is essential to look at each learning objective for the curriculum and make a determination of the best way to deliver and assess *that* objective. Ideally, the objective will be vetted from three perspectives: Is it best delivered in the classroom, asynchronously, or via a synchronous session (see Table 1-1 for comparisons of these methodologies)? Once the analysis is accomplished, the design team can mix and match the best treatment of each objective to tailor the blend that fits.

ABOUT THIS BOOK

This book follows a design team through the design and decision process for new hire training at the fictional ABC Company. The process culminates in a recommended blended solution for ABC Company's new hire sales curriculum once goals, objectives, and organizational realities have been considered.

Table 1-1. Advantages and Disadvantages of the Primary Training Delivery Methodologies

	Classroom	Asynchronous*	Synchronous
Advantages	**Individual** Training happens in one spot and in a condensed timeframe Fewer disruptions because away from desk Familiar and comfortable environment Social aspect Physical aspect Immediate access to instructor **Facilitator** Training happens in one spot and in a condensed timeframe; once class is over, facilitator often has no more responsibility Easier tracking Administratively less complex No need to learn technology to manage learning process	**Individual** Flexibility in scheduling Flexibility in location to take training Ability to review content **Facilitator** Flexibility in scheduling Flexibility in location to take facilitator's time, when used **Organization** Deployed enterprise-wide in a short period of time Easy to update content when necessary Easy to track course completion and assessments Consistency in message	**Individual** Flexibility in location to take training Learning is in shorter chunks; ability to practice or apply before moving on to next piece of content Social aspect: network building Access to a facilitator No travel Small class size **Facilitator** No travel Shorter class periods (but more frequent classes) Can develop stronger relationships with participants Small class size

	Column 1	Column 2
	Organization Training accomplished in a short period of time Short learning curve for instructors Easier tracking Administratively less complex Organization benefits of social networking among students Relatively easy to change content of curriculum when needed Able to allow for practice and application	**Organization** Travel not required Frequent offerings Shorter classes allow for more immediate application of skills More flexibility in topic choice (one- to two-hour courses are OK) Global reach; participants can be exposed to counterparts throughout the world Can reach individuals never reached before **Individual** Easy to get distracted while at own desk Can feel disconnected from instructors and peers Technology can be a barrier Small group collaboration techniques need to be taught
Disadvantages	**Individual** Time consuming Takes away from regular duties Travel may be required Overwhelming amount of information; hard to practice before moving on to the next step No access to instructor once back on the job	**Individual** Need to be self-motivated to complete Limited or no access to an instructor Easy to be distracted Technology can be a barrier

(continued on page 12)

Table 1-1. Advantages and Disadvantages of the Primary Training Delivery Methodologies (continued)

Classroom	Asynchronous*	Synchronous
Facilitator Travel may be required Difficult to ensure learning has taken place **Organization** Expensive: travel, classroom costs, time away from job Limited by number of facilitators and classrooms available	**Facilitator** When used, often required to support large class size **Organization** Depending on the technologies used can be expensive to develop and maintain Best for knowledge-only objectives; hard to incorporate practice or practical application of skills	**Facilitator** Technology can be a barrier Hard to observe or assess mastery of an objective **Organization** (Perceived) takes longer to get through curriculum Investment in technology (both classroom and possible individual stations) Limited by number of facilitators available

*Keep in mind that "asynchronous" means many different things. Some modalities are easy to implement but difficult to moderate (for example, discussion boards); others are complex to implement but easy to moderate (for example, multimedia simulations). What is implemented depends on a balance of learning goal(s), availability of technology, and budget.

Chapter 2 introduces ABC Company and the new hire sales training program that will be considered throughout the rest of the book. It uncovers the organizational goals for the proposed training redesign; analyzes the audience, work environment, and existing learning objectives; and shares the results of interviews with key stakeholders (including trainers, sales managers, and former trainees) concerning the existing training needs and training gaps.

In chapter 3, readers will have the fly-on-the-wall experience of auditing the existing training class. This incorporates an analysis of the current new hire sales training program—including a review of all materials, an observation of the class delivery, and the gathering of both trainee and manager opinions of the existing curriculum.

Chapter 4 continues to explore the new program, assuming that it will continue to be delivered in the classroom, but with a more effective design. In the long run, this will be the least expensive option for ABC Company. The learning objectives will be refined and used as the basis for the designs presented in chapters 4, 5, 6, and 7. The text will consider the design for each objective with respect to its impact on the participants, the facilitation team, the organization, and on-the-job performance.

Chapters 5 and 6 take the new learning objectives defined in chapter 4 and create an asynchronous (chapter 5) and synchronous (chapter 6) training solution that meets the needs of the participants. Again, impact on the participants, the facilitation team, the organization, and on-the-job performance will be considered when determining the treatment for each objective.

After reworking the classroom design and creating stand-alone asynchronous and synchronous designs based on refined objectives, chapter 7 combines the best of all three, and adds a few extras, to truly create the blend that fits. After the new hire sales training blend is mapped out, chapter 7 also recommends a continued training plan to help new hires meet their sales quota objectives.

Chapter 8 recommends supplemental technologies to support the blended solution. It explores mobile learning, blogs, wikis, and discussion boards with respect to learning at ABC Company. This chapter looks to the future and answers the question, "What next?"

Chapter 9 gives the reader a peek into successful blends in real organizations through the use of case studies, including a national data collection agency, a state-based health insurer, and a private firm that offers a professional certification.

Creating the blend that fits is more than picking and choosing technologies. It requires a big-picture view of the organization's business goals, the training program's learning goals, individual objectives, management support, learner aptitude, and more. Please read chapters 2 and 3 next, so that you have a solid understanding of the training program that is the basis of this book. Following chapter 3, you may choose to read the remaining chapters in any order to see how one "standard" curriculum can be adapted and delivered using an alternative delivery medium. The next chapter introduces ABC Company and the scenario that we will consider throughout the rest of the book.

Chapter 2

A Sales Training Scenario

This chapter offers a baseline narrative upon which all the subsequent chapters are built. The chapter walks you through the information-gathering process used to assess how traditional classroom training is currently conducted at ABC Company. Chapter 3 will explore the "current state" of sales training at ABC Company through a detailed classroom audit. For both of the exercises in chapters 2 and 3, imagine that you are a "fly on the wall" and follow along as key questions are posed and the information database is built to create a learning blend that fits. This chapter follows the process of

- examining the organizational goals of ABC Company
- conducting an audience and environmental analysis
- determining instructional goals and objectives
- assessing metrics and criteria for evaluation
- determining how ABC Company currently conducts sales training.

This book offers a typical scenario based on the authors' combined experience in training design—for both classroom and online environments. The purpose of this scenario is to demonstrate, in great detail, how training solution decisions are made and how, in today's workplace, blended learning is often the most effective approach.

ABC's sales training example is a good scenario because it is a familiar and popular topic and includes many basic skills that readers will be comfortable with. The course is not industry or product specific—it simply addresses the basics of sales training.

Pay close attention to the information gathered in the following analysis. These details will appear later, when decisions are made regarding the most effective training solution: classroom training, asynchronous, synchronous, or blended.

CASE STUDY SCENARIO

We will assume ABC Company has engaged a training company (the authors and you, the reader) to redesign its new hire salesperson training. The existing training is classroom based and instructor led (see chapter 3) and is offered on a monthly basis to a group of 17 to 25 individuals. The redesign has been requested, in part, because the new hires are geographically dispersed and the cost of flying them to a central training location and housing them during the two-day training class has become prohibitive. In addition, the client knows there are many more training methodologies than the classroom now in use and would like to explore all of its options. (Chapters 4, 5, and 6 will explore different delivery methodologies given the same sales training curriculum. Chapter 7 contains the final design recommendation, which includes the blend.)

ABC Company

ABC Company sells a relatively high-priced commodity ($2,500 to $6,000) in a business-to-business environment. The company is 19 years old and is still run by one of its founders. Headquartered outside of Chicago, ABC Company has 65 field offices throughout the United States. It has no formal training department; the two directors of sales training are both former sales managers of field offices and are considered subject matter experts on the topic and the company itself. These same individuals conduct the majority of the classroom-based training, which is interspersed with short appearances (two hours or less) from sales managers; contract trainers (a module on listening and questioning is conducted by a freelance trainer); and, sometimes, successful graduates of the training who come to discuss the "keys to their success."

The number of executives in the company is less than 100, the majority of whom are intermediate-level sales managers at the various field offices; slightly fewer than 1,000 salespeople are spread throughout the field offices.

The company had $6.9 million in sales last year. The average sales manager makes $100,000 per year, and salesperson compensation ranges from $35,000 to $190,000 depending on tenure with the company. Most new hires make less than $50,000 for the first two or three years until they establish a territory; however, nearly half of all new hires turn over in fewer than two years. The company hires an average of 250 new hires each year and, of that group, approximately 100 remain at the end of 24 months.

The Process—Collecting the Right Data

Before beginning any redesign effort, an understanding of the status quo is necessary. Data will need to be collected to help make decisions about design, development, and potential implementation strategies. This data collection can be loosely labeled a *needs analysis*. The needs analysis will help clarify the organizational goals for the training, the audience (trainees), the environment in which they work, the topics included in the existing training, the objectives that should be achieved, and how management determines whether or not training has been successful (assessment).

In our scenario, the first step was to conduct interviews with each of the sales training directors, a sales manager, and a recent training graduate, all of which have been transcribed below. A discussion about what was learned and what may have to be looked at more closely going forward follows each interview. This information is vital to having a complete sales training picture.

Interview with Sales Training Directors

This interview was conducted with the two directors of sales training for the company. It covered the following topics: organizational goals, audience analysis, environmental analysis, instructional goals, objectives of the training, and metrics and assessment. *Note:* Each topic begins with a definition of why knowledge in that area is important to the future design and implementation of the training.

Topic: *Organizational Goals.* All training should relate to a need or goal of the company. A need may be "to reduce on-the-job injuries" or "to increase sales by half a million this year." Understanding the business need or goal assists the designer of training in making crucial decisions about what should be included in the training.

Consultants	Sales Training Directors
What is the purpose of the training? How does it affect the organization?	The purpose of the training is to take newly hired salespeople from zero to quota in six months or less.
	Getting new hires fully functional within the first six months is critical because it means we realize a return on our investment in their training and office space. If they are not able to demonstrate that they can meet quota (and the six-month quota is not that onerous) by their eighth month of employment, then they are let go, which assists the company's bottom line by ensuring we are not continuing to invest organizational resources (salary, physical space, mileage reimbursement, administrative support, supplies) in an individual who has not been able to return that investment—it minimizes our "losses" down the road.

Topic: Audience Analysis. The audience analysis better explains who the typical participant will be. What background or previous knowledge do they have? What might be their motivation for taking the training? What do star performers do? What do poor performers do (or *not* do)?

Consultants	Sales Training Directors
What are the demographics of the typical new hire salesperson? Age? Education? Experience?	We hire people right out of college. They are typically 22 to 23 years old, and this is their first full-time job. We like this demographic because they are high energy and tenacious. They also tend to have good computer skills and demonstrate good teamwork.
	Although our salespeople do not work in teams because they are field-based representatives, we find it helpful to have team-oriented individuals who will act as unofficial mentors for the new hires. We have come to realize that this age group tends to create its own informal support group.

| How are they compensated? | They have a low base salary with commission and bonus. Salary accounts for 35 percent, and the rest is made up in commissions. They have the opportunity to earn bonuses based on certain factors such as meeting sales targets, opening new territories, and cross-selling to existing accounts. |

| How long does it take a "star" new hire to meet quota? | Our stars always meet quota by the six-month deadline. We tend to have a slow-to-start bunch that can make it by the eighth month, which is why we allow that extra two months before we make the decision to let them go. But we know that if they have not made it by the eighth month, they are never going to make quota; so it is time to cut our losses and time for them to find a job that is better suited to them. |

| What is it that impedes the individuals who do not make the six-month deadline? | We have never really done an analysis of what handicaps the non-performer, but most managers anecdotally tell us it tends to be poor time management and follow-through. It is kind of like fishing—they can get the fish on the hook, but they cannot seem to reel it in. |

| How many new hires will be in an office at one time? | Well, we offer the training once per month, so theoretically an office could have two to three new hires who have all started within the last six months. Sometimes we will have two new hires from the same office in a training class, but generally each office sponsors only one new trainee at a time. |

| What is the success rate of your new trainees? | Our fallout rate is probably 50 or 60 percent overall. About 25 percent do not make it past the eight-month mark, and then the other 25 percent or so leave of their own accord, generally before their third year with us. But that is not unusual for our industry. Sales is not an easy career. |

Topic: Environmental Analysis. An understanding of the working conditions—or environment—in which someone is asked to perform his or her job is important. Not only does it help to inform decisions about the training (you do not necessarily want people who work outside all day long to have to sit in a classroom to receive training), but it also can highlight processes in the work environment that might impede good performance—things that cannot be "fixed" by training. For instance, a company may find they experience exceptionally heavy call volume the first hour of each day, which results in poor customer service—customer service training would not fix the situation so much as extra staffing or opening the office an hour earlier.

Consultants	Sales Training Directors
Tell me about their work environment.	The salespeople work in field-based offices of which there are 65 throughout the United States. Typically there are nine to 15 salespeople per office, one administrative assistant, and one sales manager.
	They work in a radius of about 150 miles from the field office. Their typical work day starts in the office with a look at their calendar for the day, answering email and making outbound calls to follow up with prospects or current clients. By 9:30 or so, they are on the road. They are able to make anywhere from three to six sales calls in a day depending on how close the clients are and whether they are making an initial call or a full-blown presentation.
	Some salespeople return to the office at the end of the day, but others just go home.
Does the sales manager hold sales meetings?	Yes, they have a team meeting every Tuesday morning, although as I said earlier, they don't really work as a team. They are all independent representatives with their own territories and their own clientele.
What does the sales manager do to support them?	The sales manager checks in with them each morning to see what clients or prospects they are going out to see and to offer any assistance. Sometimes the manager will go out on the road with them and make calls. This is especially helpful with the new hires, who benefit from seeing how a salesperson conducts a call, the types of questions to ask, or the way to negotiate a close.

What support system exists for them once they leave training and are back on the job?

Well, the sales manager is there to answer questions and give them guidance—you know, analyze defeats and look for opportunities the new person just does not see until they have more experience. And then, as we said earlier, often a more experienced salesperson will act as a mentor and give the new hires some pointers or take him or her out on a sales call. Overall though, it is pretty much sink or swim for the new salesperson.

Topic: Instructional Goals. Instructional goals should determine what the company expects to get out of its investment in training. The instructional goal for this training is to take people right out of college and have them meet a certain sales quota by their sixth or eighth month of employment.

Consultants

What are your goals for the training program?

Sales Training Directors

The goal is to get a person, right out of school with no sales experience, up to speed selling our product within six months. This means they are able to prospect, write proposals, make presentations, negotiate, and close a sale.

Their quota is four sales within the first six months. Typically they won't close anything the first month. The really good ones will close one sale in their second or third month, but for most of them, the four sales come in months four, five, and six. That is why we said earlier we need a tenacious individual because the first few months can be exhausting and depressing—you are doing a lot of the same thing without seeing much of a return. It is an important learning experience for them, however. The more prospecting they do and initial sales calls they make, the better able they are to identify the kind of client they are able to sell to and the approach that they are most comfortable with.

Topic: Objectives of the Training. Objectives closely follow the instructional goal. Objectives are the specific knowledge or skills that need to be taught to, and mastered by, the new hire to reach the instructional goal.

Consultants

Can you list the objectives of the two-day training program?

Sales Training Directors

First and foremost they have to understand our product—what it is, what it does, how we are different from our competitors, and the value we add to an organization that purchases our product. Once they have that product knowledge under their belt, then it is all "sales" training after that:

- understanding prospecting—you know, not everyone needs what we sell
- creating a presentation
- and then, of course, presentation skills; it is not enough to put it on paper; you have to *sell* it too.

Implied in the presentation skills is handling objections, negotiating, and learning to close the sale. A lot of salespeople are unsuccessful because of one simple thing—they never ask for the sale.

Topic: Metrics and Assessment. Assessing the training will help determine if the instructional goal has been met. What behavior are the trainees exhibiting as a result of attending the training?

Consultants

So how do you assess whether or not your sales training has been effective?

Are there any assessments that occur while they are in the two-day training?

Sales Training Directors

They make four sales in six months! If they can make quota, we did our job.

Well, we have them role play and give them a paper-and-pencil quiz about the product, features, benefits, competitive advantage—that kind of thing.

Discussion. After the initial interview with the two directors of sales training, it is time to discuss what has been learned. What is working? Are there any red flags? Does more information need to be collected?

The consultants' consensus is that the training is not integrated with the actual workplace. It seems as though training is an event, which is followed by a job assignment—but the two are not purposefully joined together. Perhaps a more formal "easing in" process would help people achieve their goals faster, or stay with the company longer. In addition, the organization should consider the possibility that the sales quota is too aggressive if more than half of the new hires cannot achieve it.

Interview with a Sales Manager

The next step is to conduct an interview with a sales manager to get a fuller picture of the sales training process.

Consultants	Sales Manager
Tell me what you like to see, in terms of behavior and performance, in a new sales person.	I like someone who shows up on time and is willing to work late or on weekends. I'm willing to stay late and coach them if they are willing to come back into the office after a day on the road. I also like someone who asks a lot of questions—not only of me, but of more senior salespeople as well. That says to me that he or she can find his or her own solution; he or she isn't waiting for sales to be handed to him or her on a silver platter.
	In terms of performance, I like to see young people who can set their own schedule, who do not take disappointment or rejection personally, who conduct themselves professionally over the phone—treating an administrative assistant as well as they do the executive they are trying to get a hold of— that kind of thing.

What are the characteristics of a new hire who is able to make quota in the first six months?

Pretty much everything I just talked about. Oh! And I'd say they are very organized individuals and really good about follow-up. You know, you don't make a sale on the first call, so you have to have the discipline to follow up and go back time and time again. That takes two skills: 1) organization, because you have to make sure you schedule follow-up phone calls or meetings and 2) the confidence to follow up or try again after getting an initial "no." What we sell isn't cheap, and most people need time to think about it or budget for it; so there is definitely a period of a few months in which the new salesperson will be doing the same thing over and over without much of a result to speak of.

I guess I would say a good new salesperson is someone who understands that selling is a *process*; it is not an event.

What do you think the new hire gets from attending sales training at the home office?

They get the meat-and-potatoes stuff that I don't have time to teach them. They learn about the product, how to introduce it, how we compare with our competition—the stuff that I would have to say over and over again if I had to train every new salesperson I hire. Then, after they get those basics, I can work with them to make them salespeople.

Are you saying that the sales training does not teach them sales skills?

Whoa! Don't get me in trouble here. I think the training is good, but you can teach someone only so much in two days. Not to mention there is only so much a person who is new can absorb. They get the basics in the training, and then I mold them when they come back to me.

Do you think every sales manager approaches training new hires the same way?

That would depend on how big the office is, how many new hires they have, and how long they themselves have been a manager. One of the mistakes I see a new sales manager make is always "fixing" it for their salespeople. Rather than teaching them skills, they take over and say, "I can save this sale for you!" If the new salesperson is really perceptive, they might learn from what the sales manager does, but I don't think that happens too often. I think they end up being dependent on their sales manager rather than learning good selling skills. I mean, we are not going to win every time. That is a fact of life. People should analyze their losses and figure out if there was something else they should have done or could do in the future if they run into the same type of situation.

Discussion. The sales manager interview revealed a few pieces of information that may be critical to the effectiveness of the training, including the impression that the new hire must request further training, beyond the formal two-day class, from either the sales manager or a more senior member of the sales team. Furthermore, "training" presented by a fellow salesperson may or may not be the way the company prefers a salesperson to behave; it may be a personal technique on the part of the more senior salesperson. Apparently, each sales manager delivers further training based on his or her own belief system and availability. So while the trainees have learned about the *product* during the training class, the *process* of selling ABC's product probably varies greatly throughout the organization—something to keep in mind as we collect information and review the present training curriculum. It would be informative to analyze whether new hires who are successful in the first six months consistently come from the same field offices (this might indicate they have a different on-the-job coaching experience than new hires in other offices). One final potential red flag that has been identified from this interview is the idea that follow-through is a crucial skill to success in this profession. Is that a skill that can be taught, or is it a matter of trial and error? Perhaps the 50 percent of new hires who don't leave within the first three years have been better able to identify the need for persistence and follow-through. Again, this is something to keep in mind as information is collected to assess the current state of the sales training curriculum and process.

Interview with a Recent Sales Training Graduate

To get a complete picture of the sales training process, we conducted an interview with a recent graduate of the sales training.

Consultants	Recent Graduate
How long have you been with ABC Company?	Six months.
Have you made quota?	Not yet, but I definitely will by my eighth month!
How would you characterize your first six months on the job?	Exhausting! There is so much to learn about the product, the competition, how to sell to different types of personalities. Some people want facts and figures and paperwork, and others will listen to you for three minutes, shake your hand, and you are out of there. I have also learned that a lot of people *sound* like they are saying yes, but they really are saying no. You can't get your hopes up in this business. I have learned that a sale isn't a sale until the product is signed for at their door.
Tell us about the two days of sales training you did at the home office.	It was great! I met a lot of great new hires like myself. We got along really well, and some of us are still staying in touch, which actually is kind of helpful. It is good to know you aren't the only one going through the learning curve.

What did you learn? What has helped you back here on the job?

Well, there was a lot to take in in two days. Plus we had three or four different trainers, which was nice in a way, because it broke things up, but sometimes they seemed to contradict one another.

I think the thing I really learned from that training was to ask for help and to look for more information. For instance, if I have a question about whether our product can be operated wirelessly, I should just go to the manufacturing manuals myself. The answers are all in there, and I can find them out any time of day or night—I'm not dependent on someone in the office helping me.

How has your sales manager assisted you in your first six months on the job?

She's great! Every morning we spend five minutes or so going over what I have planned for the day, and she gives me some tips. Like yesterday, I was making my third call at a little architectural firm, and she told me it was time to ask for the sale. I have given them all the information I can, I have answered all their questions, and it was time to find out if they were just stalling me, or if they were really committed to the idea of buying. So I used the phrase she gave me: "I know you are impressed with our product and its capabilities and I know you already have ideas about how it will change your business, so I have drawn up the paperwork so that you can have it in here by the end of the month." Then I shut up and put the paperwork in front of the guy. It worked! That is how I know I'm going to make quota by my eighth month!

Congratulations! If you were to be one of the guest speakers at a future sales training session, what words of wisdom would you share?

Patience! We sell a big-ticket item, and people need time to think about buying. The six months we get to make quota is actually kind of challenging, but it can be done! I guess that is the point of a quota, isn't it? (Laughing.)

I would also tell them to use some kind of calendar system. It doesn't have to be computer based; in fact, that is one thing I really like about this job—I'm not tied to a desk and a computer. But you have to be really on top of calling people back when you say you will and following through even when you think it might be pointless. Salespeople in general do not have the best reputation, and then, you know, all of us new guys are young. I think half the time the prospect is just waiting to see if we will be back next month, or if we have run off to surf in Hawaii instead. (Laughing.)

Discussion. The discussion with the recent graduate again highlights the importance of follow-through and patience. These seem to be crucial "skills" for the new hire, and this information or skill should be transmitted in the training—if it is not already a part of the curriculum. What has come to light from this interview is that the new hires seem to create their own support network that carries on beyond the formal training class. In addition, this graduate mentioned that while the "guest speakers" were helpful in breaking up the content of the class, they seemed to deliver inconsistent messages. The guest speakers can change on a monthly basis; so it is possible each new hire class is *not* receiving the same training after all.

Is the Current Sales Training Successful?

The final bit of information gathered has to do with the current design of the training. We will determine how training is currently conducted, what topics are included, and what training processes are used, so that we have a better idea of what may or may not be working. *Note:* The client has indicated they do not necessarily want to change the content; they simply want a more expedient and modern way of delivering the content to their geographically dispersed new hires. While the existing format (classroom-based training) is expensive and cumbersome, the client is open to keeping the training class-room based so long as it is an effective delivery method. Unfortunately, the company has never done any type of training evaluation, and therefore we have no analytical data to support whether or not the existing course is truly affecting organizational goals.

The current new hire sales training class is a two-day, instructor-led training course for 17 to 25 individuals. They are flown in from their field office to the headquarters of the company. They arrive on Monday and train on Tuesday and Wednesday. The course is run once per month and is led by two former sales managers who are now the directors of sales training, and who, we have learned, have no prior experience in the training function.

The leader guide identifies these training objectives:

- Describe our basic product offering.
- Compare and contrast our product and sales platform with our three closest competitors.
- Demonstrate the ability to open a sales call and behave in a professional manner.
- Describe the characteristics of a viable prospect.
- Demonstrate good listening and questioning skills.
- Respond to objections in an appropriate manner.
- Set sales goals for self that align with quotas and sales manager expectations.

See Table 2-1 for the current agenda of the class offered by the company.

Table 2-1. Current Class Agenda

DAY 1

8:00–8:45	Welcome Introductions Housekeeping (breaks, lunch, cell phone policy, etc.) Review of the Two-Day Agenda
8:45–10:00	Product Training
10:00–10:15	BREAK
10:15–Noon	Product Training—Features and Benefits
Noon–1:00	Lunch
1:00–1:30	Our Competitive Advantage

(continued on page 30)

Table 2-1. Current Class Agenda (continued)

1:30–2:30	Presentation Skills—your dress, conduct in the client's office and on the phone, how to open the sales call
2:30–2:45	BREAK
2:45–3:45	Presentation Skills (continued) Role Play—telephone skills, initial meeting, and opening the sales call
3:45–5:00	Prospecting—who is our customer? Where do we find them?

DAY 2

8:00–8:15	Review Day 1 Questions and answers Features and Benefits "Quiz"
8:15–10:15	Listening and Questioning Skills
10:15–10:30	BREAK
10:30–Noon	Handling Objections
Noon–1:00	LUNCH
1:00–2:00	Behavioral Styles—understanding yours and the client's
2:00–4:00	Pulling It All Together—practice role plays with a 15-minute break included
4:00–5:00	Action Planning and Goal Setting
5:30–8:00	Dinner

Discussion. The fact that ABC Company has a course that is *designed* is gratifying. The training design and the objectives seem well thought out, although the agenda seems quite aggressive. We are concerned that there is not much opportunity to practice until the second day. It would be a good idea to see more information about the action planning and goal setting; perhaps this is when the new hires are told how to acquire continued training back on the job.

The company has a good solid foundation from which to start. This is not always the case. Often organizations have been teaching a class for years with no documentation or support materials—even without objectives!

CONCLUSION

A good deal of information has been gathered by analyzing the audience, the environment, and the current state of the training in regard to both curriculum and process. Some potential problems—and a number of good things—that exist in the current training have been identified.

Early in the conversations, ABC Company explained they were open to keeping a face-to-face format or going to a technologically oriented program—or something in between. As detailed in chapter 1, there are a lot of options for delivering training. The next step is to do a more in-depth analysis of the existing classroom program to ensure the objectives are valid for this company and the classroom version of this course is being delivered in the best way possible.

Chapter 3

Current Training at ABC Company

The previous chapter offered a cursory look at the current sales training program. This chapter allows you to "sit in" on a typical classroom session and explore in detail what works and what falls short. Armed with the information gathered in the previous two chapters and what is gained during the classroom audit described in this chapter, you will begin to see the opportunities for a blended solution tailored to the needs of ABC Company. This chapter examines the process of

- determining the learning objectives of the current sales training program
- reviewing and commenting on classroom materials
- determining the effectiveness of the current training.

THE COMMONALITY OF CLASSROOM TRAINING

Even with all the hype surrounding the "whiz bang" training technologies now available (see Figure 3-1), most corporate training is still delivered face to face. According to the *2007 ASTD State of the Industry Report*, 65.3 percent of all training was delivered in a traditional format in 2006, down less than

10 percent from 2001 (76 percent). If you had asked a training industry expert in 2001 what the landscape would look like in five years, the estimate of the amount of training delivered via the traditional classroom would have been a lot lower.

Figure 3-1. Emerging Modalities

Web 2.0 and emerging modalities / Company Size (percentage that use sometimes or often)				
	1 - 500 workers	501 - 5,000 workers	5,001 or more workers	Grand Total
Blogs	28.7%	19.3%	16.7%	22.0%
Learning Games	34.0%	27.5%	32.3%	31.7%
Mobile Learning	18.5%	13.8%	17.5%	16.9%
Podcasts	22.1%	19.8%	17.7%	20.0%
Simulations	51.8%	55.5%	63.6%	56.9%
Virtual labs	20.0%	21.1%	23.0%	21.4%
Wikis / Communities of Practice	33.7%	27.5%	31.8%	31.4%
Asynchronous e-Learning	79.8%	82.4%	90.5%	84.2%
Chat rooms	29.5%	21.6%	17.3%	23.1%
Classroom instruction	80.6%	93.9%	96.4%	89.7%

Reprinted with permission: The eLearning Guild Snapshot Report on Learning Modalities (2008)

As quoted during his 2003 TechLearn Conference, noted expert in learning and workplace productivity Elliott Masie said: "E-learning soon will become as ubiquitous as e-mail." A number of reasons have kept that vision from coming to pass. One of the reasons alternative delivery methods have not been adopted as quickly as anticipated is inertia; it simply is easier to deliver content the traditional way. For example, organizations commonly maintain the same training program year after year with no consideration of how that content might need to be adapted to changes in work environments, marketplace, or technologies. Often, the result is stagnant, out-of-date programs that do not contribute to individual employee performance or support current business goals. Organizations that do not have the capacity to update traditionally delivered programs do not consider new delivery formats.

Another reason for slower adoption is the information technology infrastructure of an organization, including availability of appropriate bandwidth, security protocols, and networks, which have not been able to support technology-based training initiatives. IT departments have been consumed with more "pressing" initiatives, such as data security. As time passes, these technological roadblocks are being removed, even for smaller organizations.

So while adoption has been slower than expected, more and more organizations are beginning to migrate content online, and have identified the business need to have content delivered in the most efficient way possible. Hence, organizations have displayed an increased interest in blended learning, which takes the best of all training methodologies from the perspectives of demographics, economics, and instruction.

Demographics. For the most part, the demographic factors that affect learning in the workplace concern the population of learners. Especially in today's globally diverse work environments, organizations need to make adjustments for multiple languages, various time zones, multiple generations, and cultural differences. While the content of a learning program may be the same (basic selling skills, for example), the design or delivery may have to be altered to accommodate varying demographics of the audience.

Economics. Often, training delivery options are dictated by the economics involved. For example, classroom-based training will require travel expenses, maintaining or renting classroom space, and the printing and reproduction of materials. Computer-based training options are more economical in many ways; however, they require their own set of economic decisions, such as adequate server space, the hosting of a website, or reproduction of CD-ROMs.

Instruction. The design of the actual instruction can vary greatly based on things such as individual learning styles, how immediate the need is for the training, or what access learners have to instructional methodologies. Do they have individual computer workstations? Are they able to leave their jobs to attend a four-hour or eight-hour training class?

FACTORS AFFECTING THE VALIDITY OF EXISTING TRAINING

While the client might be satisfied with the existing training content and design, he or she may not realize that, over time, even the best-designed programs tend to become less effective. This can happen for a variety of reasons:

- A successful three-day training class is compressed to two days (maybe the need for training falls within a holiday season) and happens to get positive Level 1 evaluations (see sidebar "Level 1 Evaluation Defined"). Based on these one-time reactions, the organization decides the class can be two days instead of three days in length in the future.

- New content is added because someone (a trainer, a manager) has learned of something "new" or "cool" and thinks it would fit perfectly into the training. Even though this content does not support one of the instructional objectives, it is kept in the program.
- A star in the organization is invited to be a "guest speaker." While the shared knowledge is informative, it may interfere with the timing and delivery of the planned content. When the star is not available, another might be invited; so the message changes from expert to expert.
- The first time a training program is run, the organization has formal "train the trainer" classes, including teach-back sessions and ample time for new trainers to prepare. Over time, as the instructional staff changes, the formalized structure that is used to prepare the instructors often degrades, resulting in instructors who are less prepared than their predecessors.
- Customers (internal and external) have changed—the economy may change and require different selling techniques, or the demographics of the decision maker may change. An outdated sales training course may not keep pace with a more modern culture.
- Finally, content continues to evolve (or devolve, depending on your perspective) as time moves on; anecdotes, stories, and the purpose of activities are often passed down in an "oral" history and lose their original meaning.

Ultimately, the program no longer meets all the original instructional objectives. Without periodic evaluations, deviation from the original design plan can go unnoticed.

Level 1 Evaluation Defined

According to the seminal work by Donald Kirkpatrick, there are four levels at which training can be evaluated:

- Level 1—Participant reaction
- Level 2—Participant knowledge
- Level 3—Participant behavior on the job
- Level 4—Business results or outcomes of the training.

Level 1 evaluations gather data about the participant's experience during the training and typically include questions about the experience, content, materials, and trainer.

ANALYSIS OF CURRENT TRAINING PROGRAM—A DIAGNOSTIC APPROACH

When starting to consider moving part or all of an organization's training to technologically delivered formats, designers need to determine whether the current instructional objectives, course content, and format support the ultimate learning outcomes necessary for employee success in today's market.

Our in-depth analysis of ABC Company's existing new hire sales training program will begin by auditing a class. The result of the audit will be an assessment of the training content and design to determine the best approach to achieving the learning objectives going forward. By way of the audit, an analysis of the training will include an examination of the course objectives, a review of materials, and then a detailed observation and assessment of the two-day program by the instructional design team. Each part of the analysis will conclude with a summary of recommendations for refining the design of the existing program and a list of questions for the client.

ANALYSIS OF CURRENT PROGRAM OBJECTIVES

Before observing the program in action, we need to analyze the existing course design for efficacy. The starting point is evaluating the existing learning objectives to ensure they are *instructionally sound*. By this, we mean that the objectives support the business goal and equip the participants to eventually achieve the desired level of mastery—in this case to provide ABC Company's new hire salespeople with the selling skills necessary to achieve quota in six months. Only then can we consider the content itself. The previous chapter provided the learning objectives and an outline of the course. They can be "mapped" as shown in Table 3-1.

Initial Reactions

A comparison of the objectives to the course agenda leads to the following positive observations:

- The current training design addresses many learning needs of a new salesperson.
- The role-play exercises appear to be a good opportunity for participants to put their new knowledge and skills into practice.
- The training staff includes two primary instructors plus an external vendor delivering various pieces of content. This can be very effective if the messages are well integrated.

Table 3-1. Course Outline

Objective	Agenda Topics
Describe our basic product offering.	Product Training Features and Benefits Quiz
Compare and contrast our product and sales platform with our three closest competitors.	Our Competitive Advantage
Demonstrate the ability to open a sales call and behave in a professional manner.	Presentation Skills
Describe the characteristics of a viable prospect.	Prospecting
Demonstrate good listening and questioning skills.	Listening and Questioning Skills
Respond to objections in an appropriate manner.	Handling Objections
Set sales goals for self that align with quotas and sales manager expectations.	Action Planning and Goal Setting

Some concerns include these:

- There is one agenda item—behavioral styles—that does not seem to match any of the objectives.
- The objectives are broad. For example, "Demonstrate the ability to open a sales call and behave in a professional manner," is probably better stated as two objectives ("Demonstrate . . ." and "Behave . . ."). Also, the terms *demonstrate* and *behave* are not very specific. What should we look for as a "skill" in this area? How will we know when someone is "behaving" appropriately? Similarly, the objective "Respond to objections in an appropriate manner" is rather vague.
- Listening and questioning skills are very different and would be better separated.
- The presentation skills topic includes dress, professional conduct, phone etiquette, and how to open a sales call. Opening a sales call should probably be its own agenda item.
- The final objective, "Set sales goals for self that align with quotas and sales manager expectations," implies salespeople are responsible for setting their own goals. This topic would be better expressed as "Create an action plan that helps new hires meet their sales goals."

Because salespeople do not set their own goals or quotas (as implied by the objective statement), the expectations of success for the classroom learning and the expectations back on the job might be misaligned. It is something to look out for.

- The agenda seems quite aggressive. Handling objections, a pivotal topic in most sales training classes, is allotted only 1.5 hours. Are new hires capable of mastering objections when the product knowledge is so new? Perhaps this is better relegated to a later training class.

Questions for the Client

After the initial review of the course agenda and objectives, the following questions are sent to the client:

- When and why did the behavioral styles topic get included?
- The agenda does not allow for a guest speaker (such as a stellar new hire), although in the past, these individuals have come to address the training classes. How do they fit into the curriculum? Is the agenda adjusted?
- How are the participants assessed to determine what level of knowledge and skill they have acquired? Other than the features and benefits quiz, how are things such as "respond to objections" or "demonstrate good listening skills" assessed?
- How is the learning reinforced on the job? The last topic on Day 2 is Action Planning and Goal Setting. Does this topic relate to work they will do with their manager when they get back on the job?

REVIEW OF MATERIALS

After mapping the existing content to the course objectives, we reviewed the printed materials, including

- facilitator guide
- participant guide
- slides
- handouts (product information and two role plays)
- video.

The facilitator guide and separate participant materials closely follow the content of the course and allow for participant note-taking. In addition, a review of the slides (160 in total) reveals they are visually appealing and should keep the audience's attention. The use of role plays and video should help make the training engaging.

Unfortunately, the facilitator guide is sparse, making it difficult to gauge how the topics are actually delivered. Also, while the slides are visually engaging, they are numerous. How can the facilitators address 160 slides in two days? Do they pick and choose the slides they wish to use? If so, who makes that decision and when? Can it be assumed each training class is the same as another if different people deliver the content and are allowed to choose which slides to use to illustrate their points?

Initial Reactions

The assessment of the current materials leads to the following observations:

Facilitator guide. The facilitator guide includes bullet points and reminders ("Don't forget to tell about X-advantage of Competitor Y's product"), but it is missing most details and does not include a script. The guide could be redesigned to ensure that it contains enough information and guidance so anyone, with the proper background as a salesperson or trainer, could deliver it.

Participant guide. Eighty-five percent of the participant guide is simply a replication of what appears on the slides, with some examples and anecdotes supporting the content. It also includes an extensive appendix that provides product information; contact information for the ABC Company marketing group; links to competitors' websites, with a short list of compare and contrast examples; and a list of questions commonly asked by prospects.

Slides. The slides are well designed and visually attractive, but seem to be intended for an audience of prospects, rather than a training audience. Some statistics and examples are outdated.

Handouts and collateral materials. Handouts are used for the two role plays and include the instructions for the activity and roles to be played (salesperson, prospect, and an observer). It is unclear what the observer is doing—there is no checklist for the observer to follow.

The materials supplied by the marketing department (product information) are the types of items that are left behind with prospects following an initial sales call. How they are used as an instructional tool is not clear, as they do not exactly align with the products described in the participant guide and introduced on the slides.

Video. The video effectively demonstrates good and bad examples of basic sales skills, but it is a VHS tape, and the equipment, hair styles, and office scenes are visibly dated. This can be distracting.

Questions for the Client

After the initial review of the course materials, the following questions are sent to the client:

- Because the collateral materials provided do not line up with the products discussed in the class, the client needs to verify whether or not the product information (and competitor information) in the participant guide is accurate.
- The content included in the listening and questioning topic is unclear, because it is brought in and delivered by an outside vendor. Request a copy of the materials for review.

OBSERVATION OF A LIVE TRAINING SESSION

Part three of the assessment is to observe the two-day class and evaluate its design and effectiveness. The audit will collect and assess the following information:

- The actual delivery in comparison with the planned agenda.
- The "success" of the participants in the class: What concepts came easily? What kind of questions do they have? What do they enjoy? What seems to confuse them?
- What content is actually delivered? Remember, the facilitator guide is sparse and includes mostly bulleted talking points.
- How active is the class?

Day 1 of Training

Table 3-2 illustrates the written assessment of Day 1 of training, identifying objectives and topics as they are addressed during the training schedule.

Summary of Day 1 Observation. Following the first day's observation, we summarize our remarks and include a few questions to be answered by the client.

Good:

- Ended on time.
- Loved prospecting tool.
- Demonstration room in lobby is impressive, but not used well; field trip there should be more purposeful.

Table 3-2. Day 1 Observation

Objective	Start Time	Agenda Topics	Notes and Observations Made During the Training
	8:15	Welcome	Session did not start on time because of delay getting participants' new laptops on the network.
			Most of the time was taken up by facilitators' (or trainers') and participants' introductions.
			There were two facilitators—Sam and Laura—who have been the primary teaching team for this course for the last two years.
			Housekeeping and agenda took five minutes.
Describe basic product offering	9:00	Product Training	Sam facilitated.
		Features and Benefits	Handed out collateral and gave participants 15 minutes to review (nothing planned?).
			• Identified best-selling product, highest-profit product.
		Quiz	Note: Facilitator Guide says "hand out collateral and discuss products and sales channels."
			Questions from participants:
			• Better to sell one product over another (profit versus compensation)?
			• I know I need to sell four things—four of anything?

		Facilitator spends a lot of time talking about compensation as it relates to the product. Is this appropriate for training? Can this be a reference document? Can the sales manager teach this instead? Ends on time.
10:00	Break	Break runs long—30 minutes instead of 15.
10:30	Product Training (continued)	Product training—focus on features plus benefits. Facilitator defines features versus benefits. Great activity—small group discussions using one to two pieces of collateral. Groups given 15 minutes to discuss and identify the benefits associated with the features listed in the brochures. Each group reports, and facilitator expounds. • *Needed:* place to take notes; workbook reference would be helpful. Handout at end: Top five products and their features and benefits—not part of materials we were given to review (very useful!). Who created this? • Make a job aid? *Question:* What about supplies and service contracts? When do they learn to sell those? Facilitator told them they are compensated for service agreements—but how and when do they sell that?

(continued on page 44)

Table 3-2. Day 1 Observation (continued)

Objective	Start Time	Agenda Topics	Notes and Observations Made During the Training
	Noon	Lunch	Lunch is brought in. Independent activity: Students are encouraged to go to the product demo room in the lobby to see the equipment they just learned about. *Suggestion:* Make this a formal field trip. • *Question:* Is there value in seeing and touching equipment?
Compare and contrast product and sales platform with three closest competitors	1:00 (on time)	Our Competitive Advantage	Participants are directed to appendix where web addresses appear for their three competitors and are told to surf for 20 minutes. Assignment: Find one competitive advantage (of ABC Company) and explain it to group. • 10 minutes to debrief assignment allotted—only got through three of the 19 participants. *Suggestion:* This is a great activity and participants should be given the full opportunity to present and discuss; possible to change to a small group activity to save time in the debrief. Ended on time.
Demonstrate the ability to open a sales call and behave in a professional manner	1:30	Presentation Skills	Second facilitator takes over (Laura). First time participant guide is used.

		First 20 minutes is lecture about appropriate attire, importance of business appearance because of business-to-business sales.
		Video: 10 minutes regarding telephone etiquette (off purpose?) and sales call–specific demonstrations.
		Questions from participants about how to source prospects. Facilitator needs to better make the point that these are COLD CALLS.
		Laura deflects questions until later in agenda when topic of prospecting is scheduled. She just wants to impress upon them appropriate etiquette.
2:30	Break	On time. Trainees return at 2:50.
2:50	Role play	Nineteen participants are divided into five groups of three and one group of four.
		Handout: Role play for telephone and initial sales call:
		• Use scripts in participant guide.
		• Practice with one observer who gives feedback.
		Question: How does observer know good from bad? There is no observation sheet; is it just based on video example?
		Fifteen-minute role play spent on telephone skills; remainder spent on opening first sales call.

(continued on page 46)

Table 3-2. Day 1 Observation (continued)

Objective	Start Time	Agenda Topics	Notes and Observations Made During the Training
			Observation: Opening first sales call has not been explicitly taught in the training.
			Laura circulates when called. Informal break ensues.
			Sam returns to room, and prospecting questions come up again, which he addresses with a small group who are now off-task.
Describe the characteristics of a viable prospect	4:00	Prospecting	Sam takes over.
			Observation: This topic is the best so far.
			Tool and process introduced definitive dos and don'ts.
			• *Question:* Where did this come from?
			Students love tool; ask in-depth questions.
			Follow-up: Ask Sam about the origin of this prospecting tool; what else does he have?
	5:00		End of Day 1
			Sam leaves promptly at 5:00 (he has a commitment).
			Laura takes questions from students until 5:20.

Bad:

- Facilitators seemed very focused on ending each section on time at the expense of really ensuring learning. They often ended a lesson mid-stream or failed to wrap up and provide an adequate transition to the next topic.
- Presentation skills seem mislabeled (really about dress and etiquette) and out of context with the rest of day's learning, which was more sales knowledge oriented.
- Competitive advantage activity has promise but fails to make an adequate point—seems more like "free time." The learning seemed to be lost because there was no debrief.

Questions for the Client. The following questions are sent to the client after the Day 1 review:

- Must both trainers be present both days when they don't co-facilitate (each presents his or her own topic)?
- Prospecting and features and benefits tools were great additions; can we get copies of these (not supplied with our source materials)?
- We also would like to ask all field offices what other home-grown tools they may be using (for example, presentations, leave-behinds).

Day 2 of Training

In the same manner as Table 3-2, Table 3-3 illustrates the written assessment of Day 2 of training, identifying objectives and topics as they are addressed during the training schedule.

Summary of Day 2 Observation.

Good:

- Listening and questioning presenter was good; topic was on target.
- Quiz on features and benefits was a good activity but not really a quiz and poorly placed.

Bad:

- Objections offered too soon for this audience—also too generic.
- Are behavioral styles necessary? Fluffy.

Questions for the Client. During the interview process, the facilitator explained that one of the informal outcomes of the training is a network established among the trainees. Besides the exchange of contact information, this did not happen. Is a more formalized networking plan desired? What are the goals?

Table 3-3. Day 2 Observation

Objective	Start Time	Agenda Topics	Notes and Observations Made During the Training
	8:00	Welcome, Review, Quiz	Matching quiz: Review correct answers verbally. Laura makes good points and provides good examples (she did not teach this yesterday). *Opinion:* Fun activity, but poorly placed; should come after the topic is taught. Laura introduces Paul Balboa—outside vendor (used to be a sales manager in Topeka).
Demonstrate good listening and questioning skills	8:20	Listening and Questioning Skills	Thirty minutes on listening: • 15-minute exercise (he gives NPR example) • 15-minute debrief. Questioning is second hour: • Repeats timing and process as above. • Finishes with well-produced, modern video. *Observation:* Very active, participative; students enjoy him.
	10:15	Break	On time.
Respond to objections in an appropriate manner	10:30	Handling Objections	Laura delivers; mostly lecture. *Observation:* Good topic, done well; could be better if participants had better understanding of their product.

	Behavioral Styles	Starts on time; most participants back by 12:50; Laura still delivering.
1:00		*Note:* This topic is not linked to any objective.
		Short personality survey completed in class; book *Please Understand Me* distributed. General discussion about recognizing and understanding the other person's style or preference and adapting your presentation to suit it.
2:05	Role play	Triads again; three different scenarios (law firm, hospital, school district):
		• 15 minutes individually to prep; 15 minutes to role-play and debrief
		• 1.5 hours to role-play all three scenarios
		• 30 minutes large group debrief.
		Observation: Activity runs short; participants are given "free time" essentially.
		Observation: Better observation sheet this time—can replicate for the first role play. However, those giving feedback aren't very critical or helpful; maybe need more direction about how to express feedback.
		Two hours total; including independent break (groups took break as they saw fit).

(continued on page 50)

Table 3-3. Day 2 Observation (continued)

Objective	Start Time	Agenda Topics	Notes and Observations Made During the Training
Set sales goals for self that align with quotas and sales manager expectations	4:00	Action Planning and Goal Setting	Energy is unfocused.
			Revisit information on compensation. Stories of how three to four past trainees have met their goals.
			Observation: Stories don't seem to match anything done in class in last two days (examples included calling friends, researching leases in one office building).
			Participants are asked to create a list of to-dos (action plan) and then meet with their manager about how they will implement it.
			Twenty minutes are spent on wrap-up of entire two days.
			• No questions related to content were brought up.
			• Handout of photocopied participant list (so they can stay in touch).

Suggestion. Action planning and goal setting should be addressed back on the job with each individual's sales manager, so they can be better integrated with the trainee's sales responsibilities.

CONCLUSION

The initial part of the assessment is complete. It includes data from key stakeholders, including sales trainers, sales managers, and past participants (chapter 2), and a thorough analysis of the existing training program, reviewing objectives, course outline, course materials, and course observation. Finally, the assessment includes Level 1 feedback from the participants (see Table 3-4).

Table 3-4. Level 1 Participant Evaluations of Current New Hire Sales Training

To obtain a full picture of the current training, participants who attended the audited class were asked for their reactions to the program. Out of the 19 participants who attended the class that was audited, 14 responded to the survey.

	Strongly Disagree	Disagree	Neither Agree nor Disagree	Agree	Strongly Agree
The course material was clearly and logically laid out.	0	1	1	7	5
The activities helped me to understand my role as a salesperson.	0	1	1	9	3
The workbook was clearly laid out and easy to follow.	0	1	1	7	5
The workbook supported my learning process, providing enough information and enough note-taking space.	0	1	1	7	5

(continued on page 52)

Table 3-4. Level 1 Participant Evaluations of Current New Hire Sales Training (continued)

I will be able to use the workbook back on the job.	0	0	4	4	6
I understand ABC Company's product offerings.	0	1	3	7	3
I feel confident in my ability to source prospects for the products and services I sell.	0	0	3	7	4
I feel confident about going out on my first sales call. I understand how to open a call and probe for an opportunity.	1	0	4	6	3
I understand the common objections to our products and service offerings and how to respond appropriately.	0	0	2	10	2

	Too Fast	Just Right	Too Slow
The pace of the course was	3	10	1

The most significant thing learned in this training program was:

About the products

How to probe for opportunity

Product line

Be prepared, know your stuff, network with colleagues

Do research on customer before approaching

How to head out to my first sales call!

I feel ready to go out and sell!!

Sales strategies

Product line and specs

How to ask questions

How to make a pitch

The differences between our products and our competitors' products

Learning our competitors' product offerings

The one thing I would like more training on is:

Comparing ABC's product line with competitors' products

Overcoming objections

Sales skills

Features and functionality of some of the products

Follow-up process

I need to practice with the product more to feel confident about presenting it as a solution

Sales strategies

I am not comfortable with the calling process—do not feel I am ready

Prospecting

More on sales skills

Still learning the common objections to our product offerings—internalizing this for automatic and quick response

None

Please provide additional comments on any aspect of the training you would like to bring to our attention:

The facilitators were amazing!

The training was very intense; I would prefer to have it spread out over several weeks instead of so much information presented in two long days.

This was information overload. My brain couldn't take it all in over a two-day period.

Great class! Great instructors!

Thank you. I enjoyed the class.

RE: "workbook was aligned with what the trainer was speaking about and/or the slides." TOO MUCH! Trainers didn't do anything but basically read the workbook or slides to us. Material was often redundant and much time would have been better spent just letting us read than being read to.

Would like more opportunities for hands-on time with the actual products.

Good facilitators. Not sure I can apply all of it back on the job.
Good reinforcement of best practices.
A lot of information in a short amount of time.
Thank you for taking the time to provide this information and practice.

The next chapter will demonstrate how we use all the information gathered up to this point to redesign ABC Company's classroom instruction—which is our first deliverable to the client.

Chapter 4

A New Classroom Approach

This is the first of four chapters that will introduce various approaches to redesigning ABC Company's existing classroom-based new hire sales training program, beginning with a traditional classroom approach in this chapter. Chapters 5, 6, and 7 will address three other delivery methodologies: asynchronous; synchronous; and, finally, a blend of all four primary delivery mediums.

Note that each delivery method will be analyzed from the perspective of the participant, the facilitator team, and the sponsoring organization. In addition, all the scenarios take into account design implications (such as the need to purchase or create a video), impact on the job, or changes in the assessment plan that may result as methodologies change. See sidebars "Stakeholder Needs" and "Impact of Choices" for a description of why these elements must be taken into account to build effective training, no matter how it is delivered.

REDESIGN OF THE CLASSROOM-BASED TRAINING

As we focus on redesigning the current classroom training program, remember that the client, at this point, believes the training will continue to be delivered in the classroom. Based on the analysis done in chapter 2, the objectives and expected training outcomes have been adjusted to be more specific and demonstrable. Because the success of any training is based on an assessment,

---

Stakeholder Needs

Understanding the needs of the three key stakeholders in the redesigned sales training is key to the process. Here is a description of each stakeholder group considered as part of the design scenarios described in this chapter:

- **The participants.** Different delivery methods will affect the training audience in different ways. For instance, a classroom-based design is interactive and allows participants to learn from the instructor as well as from the experiences of other individuals in the class. However, an asynchronous class typically does not have any human interaction and is dependent on a participant being self-directed and motivated—finishing the training class is entirely up to the learner.
- **The facilitator team.** Because almost everyone has gone to school for 12 or more years, everyone is familiar with the role of a facilitator in the classroom; but what is the role of the facilitator if he or she is not actually leading a "class"? For example, will the two facilitators for ABC Company have a role should the organization choose to deliver the training in a different format? If they *do* have a role, what will that role be?
- **The sponsoring organization.** Regardless of the delivery medium, training is a large monetary investment for any organization. There are financial and organizational pros and cons to be considered when deciding the best delivery method for a training offering. For example, with e-learning, the initial investment is typically more costly than designing and rolling out a comparable classroom-based course, but it can be delivered to a wider audience in less time. An e-learning course can be the most economical approach, depending on the organizational constraints such as number of employees needing training or how quickly information must be disseminated.

---

each training objective is now stated in a way that can be measured. In addition, sub-objectives for each main objective have been defined so the participant has a better understanding of what will be taught in each topical area.

The nine objectives that all delivery methodologies will fulfill in the learning solutions described in chapters 4 through 7 include the following:

- **Objective 1:** Represent the organization in a professional manner.
- **Objective 2:** Describe the features and benefits of the company's five core products to prospective buyers.

Impact of Choices

Depending on the delivery method, designers must consider how these choices influence design, desired impact on the job, and any assessment plan.

- **Design implications.** Different delivery methods will change the design of the course. A classroom-based course can be very interactive and can include group activities in the design. However, an asynchronous course would determine whether the interaction or activity is crucial to the learning, and if not, then determine how the same learning outcome could be achieved by an independent learner.
- **Impact on the job.** Ultimately, any training program should enable participants to return to their jobs and implement what they have learned during the training. To accomplish this, the learning must be designed in a way that is immediately applicable on the job, and the participant must be motivated to use the new knowledge and skills.

  For example, in a classroom-based training course, a follow-on activity might be for the facilitators to check in with the participants once a week to see what kind of success they are having implementing their new knowledge and skills back on the job, as well as to offer support and coaching. However, if the training course is designed to be offered asynchronously, the coaching may have to be offered by the participant's sales manager or a more senior salesperson in the office. While the same objective can be met, the methodology for meeting that objective might be quite different.
- **The assessment plan.** If the ultimate goal is to have an individual return to the job prepared to implement new knowledge and skills, then there should be some way of assessing whether the training has been successful in accomplishing that goal. Currently the new hire sales training offered by ABC Company does not include any type of on-the-job assessment plan; this is a critical element that will be added to the curriculum regardless of the delivery method. Similar to on-the-job considerations, assessment approaches might differ depending on how the training is delivered. Therefore, the assessment for each objective will be defined once the training approach has been determined.

- **Objective 3:** Compare and contrast the company's core products with the products of our three closest competitors.
- **Objective 4:** Target high-potential prospects.
- **Objective 5:** Demonstrate the ability to open a sales call.
- **Objective 6:** Demonstrate the ability to manage a prospect meeting.
- **Objective 7:** Demonstrate the ability to close a sales call.
- **Objective 8:** Manage objections.
- **Objective 9:** Implement an action plan designed to meet quota in the specified time period.

NEWLY DESIGNED OBJECTIVES AND DESIGN CONSIDERATIONS

In the detailed discussion of each objective, you will find a table that includes the following elements: the old objective as stated in chapter 2; the new objective, with sub-objectives, which have been designed in accordance with the new expectations for learning outcomes; and the rationale for the newly designed objective, which will provide you some insight into the purpose of the objective. We then offer a discussion on the design approach for the classroom-based delivery methodology as well as the resultant implications for participants, design, facilitators, the organization, the job, and the assessment plan. If an objective has been added as entirely new, the old objective column will say "See new objective."

Objective 1

Table 4-1 illustrates Objective 1: Represent the organization in a professional manner.

Classroom Design Approach. The course will assign a pre-work assignment that asks attendees to prepare a short introduction about themselves, including their name, what field office they are from, where they went to college (because most participants are recent college graduates), and perhaps what they already know about the product and the services they will be selling. The pre-work instructions also will tell them to dress professionally and alert them to the expectation that their fellow participants will be critiquing their presentation. An observation form will be created for the participants who are in the "audience," so that they can evaluate one another on their chosen attire, their skill at delivering information to strangers, and whether or not they make eye contact (see sidebar "Observation Form for Presentations"). Throughout the day, a facilitator will take participants one at a time to a

Table 4-1. Represent the Organization in a Professional Manner

Old Objective	New Objective	Rationale
See new objective.	1. Represent the organization in a professional manner. 1.1 Define professionalism. 1.2 Select attire that conforms to company guidelines. 1.3 Develop rapport. 1.4 Utilize body language and eye contact in a way that creates a comfortable environment.	This objective was culled from the old objective, which stated: Demonstrate the ability to open a sales call and *behave in a professional manner.* This objective was created as a stand-alone objective because behaving in a professional manner should be a core skill regardless of what task an individual is performing. The organization considers this an important objective to call out and practice because the majority of new hires come directly from college and have limited professional experience.

private room for a five-minute coaching conversation based on the collective feedback.

Impact on Participants. This approach to introductions helps the participants jump right into the topic. It is a relatively realistic experience because, in the course of a salesperson's career, he or she will make many presentations to individuals without first having a relationship with them. This approach also gives the participants the ability to demonstrate how serious they are about succeeding on the job by showing how prepared they are for their presentation. While this might be an intimidating introduction to the class and new colleagues, most of them should have had enough experience in college with oral presentations to be successful.

Observation Form for Presentations

Instructions: Check yes or no for each question and provide comments as you deem appropriate. Keep in mind that you are assisting your fellow participant who, in turn, will assist you with feedback as well.

Eye contact

Did the presenter:

	Yes	No	Comments
Make eye contact with the whole room?			
Make sustained eye contact with individuals (more than three seconds)?			

Body Language

Did the presenter:

	Yes	No	Comments
Have any nervous habits? If yes, please describe.			
Stand in a way that commanded attention?			
Stand in a way that was distracting?			

Vocal Ability

Did the presenter:

	Yes	No	Comments
Speak clearly?			
Articulate clearly?			
Use words that were easily understood by the audience?			
Have a well-rounded vocabulary?			
Have any vocal "crutches" ("um, ah, ya know")?			

Impact on Design. An experiential activity has more impact than listening to a lecture about appropriate dress, eye contact, and behavior. In addition, hearing their fellow participants' feedback about their mannerisms or appropriateness of dress will have a long-lasting effect on each individual. Advanced communication with participants will be required to allow them to prepare for their introductory presentations.

Impact on Facilitation Team. The old ABC Company training design used a lecture approach that relied on the facilitator providing content. This new trainee presentation activity places the onus on the participant to demonstrate understanding of the content, permitting the facilitator to move into the role of "coach" to provide feedback.

Impact on the Organization. Contacting attendees in advance of the training and providing them with instructions on how to prepare for their first presentation will require a bit more coordination than in the past, but it should not be cumbersome. Communicated strategically, this approach can send a message to the participants that there are high expectations for their performance right from the start.

Impact on the Job. This process closely emulates what the salespeople will be doing on a day-to-day basis. They will constantly meet new individuals and be required to give presentations, and this exercise gives them an opportunity to practice.

Assessment Plan. Fellow participants will assess participant introductions, using a checklist of observations. The facilitators will then gather the feedback and meet with each individual over the course of the two days of training to review the feedback and offer pointers for improvement. For example, a participant who uses "um" and "ah" frequently will be coached to pause and say nothing rather than fill the space with a nonsense word. Because one of the instructions and expectations is that the participants will select attire that conforms to company policy, the presentation also will assess whether or not the person has read and understood company policy (which facilitators will need to provide to them in advance of the training).

While this form of assessment is informal, obtaining feedback from 15 or more fellow participants will be much more beneficial than quizzing individuals about whether or not they can define *professionalism* or asking them about the importance of eye contact when addressing an audience.

Objective 2

Table 4-2 illustrates Objective 2: Describe the features and benefits of the company's five core products to prospective buyers.

Table 4-2. Describe the Features and Benefits of the Company's Five Core Products to Prospective Buyers

Old Objective	New Objective	Rationale
Describe our basic product offering.	2. Describe the features and benefits of the company's five core products to prospective buyers. 2.1 What are the features and benefits? 2.2 What are ABC Company's core products? 2.3 What are features and benefits of the core products? 2.4 Identify which product most closely aligns with a prospect's needs.	The original objective was vague and incomplete. What is meant by "describe"? To whom? What should be included? Does each prospect receive the same description? Also, the phrase "basic product offering" was left to interpretation. The company carries more than 30 products—which are to be considered "basic"? The new objective addresses these questions.

Classroom Design Approach. Facilitators will address this topic using slides that depict the actual products as well as pictures with callouts of the features and benefits of each product in the workbook. New hires cannot be expected to master information on 30 different products; so this introductory sales training course will focus on the five top-selling products. Each product will be discussed in terms of features and benefits to the end user. The workbook will contain a checklist that matches potential prospect needs to ABC Company's core product set. For instance, a company with fewer than 1,500 employees would benefit more from Product A, while a company with more than 1,500 employees would benefit from the features of Product B. This checklist will help the participants internalize how aligning a prospect's needs with the product will help them personalize their sales call.

Once the products are reviewed in class, a "field trip" to the showroom in the lobby will allow participants to view and handle the products that are on display. The students will bring their workbooks to the showroom so that they can compare the pictures of the products with the actual products, and make additional notes that will assist them in explaining the products to prospects and clients.

The expectation for this objective is simple recognition and recall of the five products and their major features and benefits.

Impact on Participants. The participants will have the opportunity to view and handle the actual products while making notes that will assist them on the job. The workbook pictures and pages will function as a beneficial reference for them as well as serve as a model of the type of information they will need to collect in the future, on their own, as they learn about the company's additional 25 products.

Impact on Design. This is a very straightforward activity encompassing pictures of the products and their significant features and benefits from the prospect's perspective. Training designers will need to develop a checklist to match ABC Company's features and benefits to a potential prospect's needs.

Impact on Facilitation Team. Delivering content in this manner is time-consuming and redundant. The content delivery does not necessarily require an instructor; however, participants may have questions about how to sell or pitch a particular product, and having a facilitator lead this content is a good idea. This delivery process aligns closely with how the facilitators currently conduct the training class, so they will be comfortable delivering this information.

Impact on the Organization. For the organization to be successful, salespeople must understand the top products on which to focus their energy, including the features and benefits of each, as well as how to sell the product to a prospect who has expressed a particular need.

Impact on the Job. One's performance on the job is completely dependent on understanding ABC Company's product offerings and how they differ from one another. In the future, participants will be required to acquire the knowledge about the remaining products on their own; so they will have to understand where to access information and how to interpret product specifications and other details to identify the features and benefits of the entire ABC Company product line.

Assessment Plan. This objective will be assessed in a written format. First, participants will be given a picture of each of the products and asked to label the key features; then they will write a short description of the benefits associated with each feature. Afterward, the facilitator will present the participants with typical customer scenarios and ask them to choose the correct product to meet the customer's needs. It is impossible for the assessment to be all-encompassing, as every customer's needs and utilization will be different. Therefore, this assessment method will help the participants understand the process of listening to a client's needs and expectations and aligning them with the features and benefits of one of the company's products or services.

Objective 3

Table 4-3 illustrates Objective 3: Compare and contrast the company's core products with the products of our three closest competitors.

Table 4-3. Compare and Contrast the Company's Core Products With the Products of Our Three Closest Competitors

Old Objective	New Objective	Rationale
Compare and contrast our product and sales platform with our three closest competitors.	3. Compare and contrast the company's core products with the products of our three closest competitors. 3.1 Identify closest competitors, including characteristics that define them as closest competitors. 3.2 Identify competitor offerings that most closely align with our own. 3.3 Compare similarities and contrast differences between the competitor's products and our core products.	The original objective contained jargon ("sales platform") that not even the sales managers could define; so that language was removed. In addition, it is ambitious to assume that new hires can leave the program being able to discuss more than 30 products; so the objective now references the core products, identified in Objective 2.

Classroom Design Approach. With a basic understanding of ABC Company's product offerings, the participants will now spend time independently researching ABC Company's three biggest competitors and their product offerings. Each participant will be asked to research just one competitor, and after 20 minutes of independent research on the Internet, all participants who had the same competitor will be given another 10 minutes to work together as a small group to compare what they learned about the competitor's product and make a presentation to the larger group. A job aid will be given to each participant to provide focus while doing their Internet research (see sidebar "Job Aid Defined"). After each group makes its presentation to the larger group, a facilitator will discuss key points that were not addressed by the participants. During the course of the independent research and small-group activity, the two facilitators will circulate throughout the room offering assistance as necessary.

> ### Job Aid Defined
>
> A job aid is a quickly accessed reference sheet designed to help the user complete a task or process. It can be used as reinforcement for training, or it may be used in lieu of training (as in the job aid that assists every office worker to change the toner in the photocopier without ever having to take a training class in toner-changing).

Impact on Participants. This activity prepares salespeople to be ready to react when a competitor introduces a new product. The process will train them to look for certain features of a competitor's product and compare them with ABC Company's offerings.

Impact on Design. Participants will use a job aid, which will provide direction for their Internet research (see sidebar "Competitor Research"). The job aid will provide guidelines on how to research a competitor, as well as provide space for answers to specific questions (for example, "How many products does a competitor have, and how do they align with the product line of ABC Company?" and "Identify the products that are most closely aligned with ABC's core products, and how those products are similar or different."). During the small group activity, the participants will be tasked with designing a presentation to address similarities between products and how ABC's products can be considered to be superior (for example, "What is it about ABC Company's product that is similar but clearly superior to the competition?"). This activity will not only reinforce features and benefits but also assist participants in learning to overcome objections, which will be taught later in the curriculum.

Impact on Facilitation Team. Rather than simply lecture and hope participants absorb what they need to know about the competition, facilitators of this process will begin to train participants to be self-sufficient (research on their own) and to rely on co-workers (small group activity). The facilitator's role will be to correct or clarify any misconceptions during the small group presentations and also to provide any additional insight into the competitor

---

Competitor Research

Name of company: _____

Market that they serve: _____

How is their market similar to, or different from, ABC Company's market?

_____

How many products do they carry? _____

Which products do they promote most heavily? (Name them.)

_____

_____

_____

_____

_____

How does each of the above-named products align with our products?

_____ is most like _____

_____ is most like _____

_____ is most like _____

_____ is most like _____

_____ is most like _____

---

that is not readily apparent from Internet research (for example, "Product X was on the market for only 18 months and had serious maintenance issues; if you find a prospect who still owns Product X, suggest how much money can be saved in the first year by ABC Company's warranty and reliability of comparable Product L.").

Impact on the Organization. This process will teach new salespeople self-sufficiency and how to rely on a network of peers.

Impact on the Job. The job aid will be designed to provide structure for research done back in the office, and participants will be able to download copies, as needed, for their own individual research needs.

Assessment Plan. This objective will not be assessed as much as it will be reinforced by the new hire's manager once the new hire returns to the job. An individual will need to practice this skill regularly for it to be mastered.

Objective 4

Table 4-4 illustrates Objective 4: Target high-potential prospects.

Table 4-4. Target High-Potential Prospects

Old Objective	New Objective	Rationale
Describe the characteristics of a viable prospect.	4. Target high-potential prospects. 4.1 Describe the characteristics of a viable prospect. 4.2 Develop a prioritized prospecting list. 4.3 Create a customized approach to engage the prospect in a sales conversation.	The original objective did not take this concept far enough. A salesperson must do more then describe a viable prospect; he or she must identify prospects and then find a way to engage them.

Classroom Design Approach. This topic will be based on a Profiling and Qualifying Tool (see sidebar "ABC Company's Profiling and Qualifying Tool") that was created by one of the facilitators to support the existing classroom design. The tool helps participants profile ideal prospects. This topic will enable the new salespeople to understand that not all prospects are viable customers. The tool will discuss such things as minimum employee size, minimum number of locations considered to be ideal in a prospect, and parameters for company earnings. Once the basic concept has been reviewed, participants will be given a handout that contains profiles of 10 potential prospects, and using the tool, they will prioritize the prospects to categorize those that are most likely to need ABC Company's products *and* buy from the organization. This independent "ideal prospect" activity will be followed by a large group debrief, so that participants can compare their lists and their rationale for ordering their lists.

Impact on Participants. As with the previous objectives, the expectation is that the new hire salespeople will be able to be self-sufficient once they return to their field offices and are assigned a territory. The prospecting tool and the

ABC Company's Profiling and Qualifying Tool

Note: Much of the information needed to complete this form cannot be gathered without an initial call to the prospect.

Company name: _____

Number of locations: _____

Contact's name: _____

Number of employees: _____ (in total) _____ (at each location)

Are they currently using a competitor's product or service? ❏ Yes ❏ No

If yes, who? _____

Instructions: Using the following ideal prospect checklist, circle the appropriate number in the row opposite the statement you see in the left column. By awarding points to each aspect of the prospect's business, you can create a better profile of whether or not the prospect is a quality lead.

Ideal Prospect Criteria	Don't Know/Not Applicable	Does Not Meet Criteria		Meets Criteria Somewhat		Exactly Meets Criteria
The Company						
More than 2,500 employees	0	1	2	3	4	5
More than one local location (100-mile radius)	0	1	2	3	4	5
More than $2 million in annual net sales	0	1	2	3	4	5
Centralized purchasing location	0	1	2	3	4	5

Currently our customer or does business with one of our top three competitors	0	1	2	3	4	5
Leases rather than buys equipment	0	1	2	3	4	5
The Individual You Are Dealing With						
Concerned with efficiency and productivity	0	1	2	3	4	5
Concerned with ease-of-use	0	1	2	3	4	5
Understands value-added concept	0	1	2	3	4	5
Needs to make decision within six months	0	1	2	3	4	5

Scoring: The "ideal customer" will have a score of 40 or more:
40–50: This is a quality lead.
30–39: Simply a longer sale, but you should start making inroads.
20–29: Return to the prospect next year and reevaluate.
19 or less: Do not pursue this prospect.

thought process that is involved in the prioritization of the prospect examples will help participants understand the questions they should ask and the decisions they should make to maximize their selling time and have the most success with closing sales.

Impact on Design. The tool has already been created, thanks to one of the facilitators, but it may need to be tweaked a bit once the ideal prospect characteristics are vetted with a number of field office managers. The profiles handout will need to be created from scratch, but this should not be difficult, as every sales manager would certainly have a client that could be profiled in this manner.

Impact on Facilitation Team. The delivery of this topic is something that the facilitator, Sam, is already familiar with, as he uses the tool in the current classroom design when speaking about the topic of prospecting. In the new design, the facilitators will circulate throughout the training room while the students are completing the independent activity. Facilitators will need to understand the "correct" order of the prospect list and the rationale behind that order to help participants better understand the decisions they will have to make when choosing whether or not to pursue a prospect.

Impact on the Organization. This learning process is ideal for helping the new salespeople become independent and successful earlier in their sales careers.

Impact on the Job. The profiling process should enable new salespeople to succeed more quickly because they are pursuing only qualified leads.

Assessment Plan. This topic will not be formally assessed, as it would be difficult to determine if someone truly has the critical skills necessary to identify good prospects until he or she has been on the job for at least two months and has had the opportunity to research and profile a number of prospects in a given territory.

Objective 5

Table 4-5 illustrates Objective 5: Demonstrate the ability to open a sales call.

Table 4-5. Demonstrate the Ability to Open a Sales Call

Old Objective	New Objective	Rationale
Demonstrate the ability to open a sales call and behave in a professional manner.	5. Demonstrate the ability to open a sales call. 5.1 Greet the prospect. 5.2 Propose an agenda for the meeting, state the value to the prospect, and check that the prospect accepts your agenda. 5.3 Ask questions that uncover the prospect's true need.	"Behave in a professional manner" was determined to be an independent objective and is now addressed in Objective 1. The steps involved in opening a sales call are now defined so that they can be more clearly assessed.

Classroom Design Approach. This topic will be taught via the use of a video and a role play. Participants will watch five vignettes of salespeople opening various sales calls with potential clients. A short discussion will follow each vignette covering what the salesperson demonstrated, how it was received by the prospect, and why that might be a good initial opening to a sales call. Once the participants feel confident about the process of opening a sales call, they will break into groups of three to role-play this skill. Each individual will practice opening a sales call twice. When not practicing in the role of salesperson, the other trainees in each team will either play the role of the prospect or make notes as an observer of the practice interaction.

Following the role play, a large group discussion will be conducted asking the participants to brainstorm questions to uncover a prospect's needs. The participants will use their workbooks to make note of the appropriate types of questions used to uncover a prospect's needs. A short lecture will explore the difference between open-ended and closed-ended questions.

Impact on Participants. Not only will the participants be able to see appropriate sales call opening techniques modeled by various individuals in different situations, they also will be able to practice emulating the same techniques themselves. This approach gives them a number of best practice examples as well as the opportunity to internalize the process and the dialogue via role-playing. The final activity, brainstorming appropriate questions, will assist new salespeople in getting to the next level. A good opening dialogue is not enough; the salesperson also must know what kinds of questions to ask and what kind of information to gather from a prospect to make an informed decision about whether or not to continue to pursue the prospect.

Impact on Design. Designers will purchase a commercial video that demonstrates opening and closing a sales call. In addition, they will create role-play roles and an observation checklist.

Impact on Facilitation Team. This training approach is particularly beneficial for the facilitators because, while this topic certainly could be taught in lecture format or the two facilitators themselves could demonstrate appropriate sales call openings, seeing a number of examples and a number of different approaches, as portrayed in the video, has much more impact. The facilitators will need to be skilled at the debriefing of each vignette to clearly call to the participants' attention the process and technique each vignette demonstrates. They also will need to be available to circulate throughout the training room to assist the teams during the practice role plays to ensure that they stay on task and are practicing the appropriate dialogue correctly.

Impact on the Organization. The organization will benefit from salespeople who have had an opportunity to practice this skill before opening a sales call with an actual prospect.

Impact on the Job. Opening a sales call and being able to interact with various personality styles of business people is a technique that can be perfected only with practice and time. The participants' ability to practice during the role play will be beneficial but will not be extensive enough to allow them to truly master opening a sales call. The list of questions will be a handy reference for new hires once they are back on the job.

Assessment Plan. The role play serves as an assessment because it gives each individual the ability to demonstrate his or her understanding of the required skills and receive feedback from a fellow participant. The feedback form that is used during the training may also be forwarded to an individual sales manager, so that the manager can continue to assess and hone the skills of each new hire assigned to his or her office.

Objective 6

Table 4-6 illustrates Objective 6: Demonstrate the ability to manage a prospect meeting.

Table 4-6. Demonstrate the Ability to Manage a Prospect Meeting

Old Objective	New Objective	Rationale
See new objective.	6. Demonstrate the ability to manage a prospect meeting. 6.1 Probe for clarification. 6.2 Suggest solutions that meet the need.	This objective was added because, effectively, the course had been teaching salespeople enough to get in the door, but not providing them the skills they needed after they arrived. The new objective attempts to assist salespeople in managing the meeting and working with the prospect to devise a solution that ultimately results in a sale.

Classroom Design Approach. This topic is, in essence, a continuation of the prior topic. It now asks participants to put together their ability to ask appropriate questions to gain more information about the prospect and his or her organization, and then suggest an ABC product or service that meets the needs of the prospect.

The participants will work in triads. Each triad will be provided with a completed Profiling and Qualifying Tool for a representative company and will create a strategy to manage the meeting. The groups will spend five minutes determining:

- The goals for the meeting (get the sale, get a meeting with a different department, set up a second meeting)
- Questions that need to be answered by the prospect
- A strategy for keeping the prospect's interest throughout the sales call.

Each group will then present their approach to the class, and receive feedback and advice to strengthen their strategies.

Impact on Participants. This is a very experiential approach, which will allow participants to think strategically and apply what they have learned early in the class.

Impact on Design. At least six completed profiles will need to be developed—one for each triad group.

Impact on Facilitation Team. The facilitators will provide feedback during the group presentations, taking the point of view of potential prospects.

Impact on the Organization. The organization will have a more confident salesforce that understands more completely the nature of the sales process.

Impact on the Job. This process should lead to more closed sales because the salesperson will understand how to maintain an effective dialogue with a prospect.

Assessment Plan. The presentation(s) will inform the facilitators as to the level of audience understanding.

Objective 7

Table 4-7 illustrates Objective 7: Demonstrate the ability to close a sales call.

Classroom Design Approach. Most often a sale is lost simply because a salesperson never asks for the sale. This topic culminates the sales call process by teaching participants how to successfully close a sale. A video of sales closing vignettes will be used, and each vignette will be debriefed, as in Objective 5, to help the participants understand the dialogue they might hear that indicates a prospect is willing to close the sales process. A final round

Table 4-7. Demonstrate the Ability to Close a Sales Call

Old Objective	New Objective	Rationale
See new objective.	7. Demonstrate the ability to close a sales call. 7.1 Confirm that the meeting has met the prospect's expectation. 7.2 Close the call with suggested next steps and timelines.	This new objective is included to ensure that a salesperson can effectively close a sales call. This was not addressed in the original training.

of role plays will be conducted, which will assist the participants in bringing together the entire process: opening a sales call, gathering information by asking appropriate questions, offering solutions by targeting specific products or services to the prospect's expressed needs, and finally asking for the sale and suggesting next steps.

Impact on Participants. Participants will see and hear best practices and dissect them for the techniques that they should emulate themselves. They will then be able to practice the entire sales call process from beginning to end, which will help them to understand and internalize their role in the sales call process.

Impact on Design. This is effectively the same exercise that was used when addressing Objective 5, and the same video will be utilized. Again, role-play roles and an observation checklist will need to be created.

Impact on Facilitation Team. The facilitators will need to be skilled at the debriefing of each vignette to clearly call to the participants' attention the process and technique each vignette demonstrates. They also will need to be available to circulate throughout the training room to assist the teams during the practice role plays to ensure that they stay on task and are practicing the appropriate dialogue correctly.

Impact on the Organization. The organization will benefit from salespeople who have had an opportunity to practice this skill before closing a sales call with an actual prospect.

Impact on the Job. The participants' ability to practice during the role play will be beneficial but will not be extensive enough to allow them to truly master closing a sales call.

Assessment Plan. The role play serves as an assessment because it gives each individual the ability to demonstrate his or her understanding of the required skills, and to receive feedback from a fellow participant. The feedback form that is used during the training may also be forwarded to an individual sales manager, so that the manager can continue to assess and hone the skills of each new hire that comes into his or her office.

Objective 8

Table 4-8 illustrates Objective 8: Manage objections.

Table 4-8. Manage Objections

Old Objective	New Objective	Rationale
Respond to objections in an appropriate manner.	8. Manage objections. 8.1 Identify an objection. 8.2 Categorize the objection. 8.3 Respond to the objection in a way that keeps the conversation moving forward.	This objective was reworded to align with Objectives 6 and 7.

Classroom Design Approach. This topic will be presented in a "game" format, requiring participants to call on their knowledge of ABC Company's products and services, their features and benefits, and how they would best align with an individual's expressed needs to respond to typical objections they will hear on the job.

The participants will be divided into four groups. Each group will be tasked with articulating five objections in a particular category such as time, budget, and internal reorganization. Each team will then pose one of their objections to all three of the other teams, who will then have one minute to come up with an appropriate response that will enable the dialogue with the prospect to continue. The team that posed the question will choose the winning team and explain why they chose that response as the winner. The facilitators will add suggestions or correct misinformation, if necessary, during the explanatory process. The process will continue until each team has delivered all their objections to the other teams.

Impact on Participants. This process requires participants to begin to look at the ABC sales process from the perspective of a prospect or client and to anticipate objections they might hear while on the job. It also allows them to rely on one another to come up with appropriate answers.

Impact on Design. This training approach requires minimal design other than a set of guidelines by which each team is to create its objections and rules for the "game" itself.

Impact on Facilitation Team. The facilitators act as coaches who correct behaviors or dialogue as necessary.

Impact on the Organization. The activity forces participants to consider the prospect's perspective, which in turn creates a more informed and, therefore, effective salesperson.

Impact on the Job. Having participants work together to resolve common problems in the sales process will teach them to rely on one another as a support network once they are on the job.

Assessment Plan. This skill will be assessed on the job once participants are interacting with true prospects. The assessment will be conducted by the salesperson's manager after observing a sales call. The sales managers will be provided with instructions on how to manage this assessment.

Objective 9

Table 4-9 illustrates Objective 9: Implement an action plan designed to meet quota in the specified time period.

Classroom Design Approach. This topic will begin with a field office sales manager discussing the sales goal process. Topics include how quotas are assigned, the typical success trajectory of a new salesperson, time management best practices, and the compensation system. The participants will be encouraged to ask questions regarding their role and the expectations of the sales managers. This will be an informal discussion to allow participants to be comfortable with someone in a management role and begin to see them as a coach and a support system rather than as a task assigner or school principal.

The sales manager will then discuss how he or she would approach working with a new hire. The ideal situation would be for one of the training participants to eventually end up in this sales manager's office; the manager could then begin to work one-on-one with that individual, demonstrating how the goal-setting and mentoring process would be undertaken. Participants will be given 20 to 30 minutes to create an individual action plan based on the expectations of the guest speaker (manager) and to plan a conversation with their managers for the first week that they are on the job.

Table 4-9. Implement an Action Plan Designed to Meet Quota in the Specified Time Period

Old Objective	New Objective	Rationale
Set sales goals for self that align with quotas and sales manager expectations.	9. Implement an action plan designed to meet quota in the specified time period. 9.1 Articulate quota requirements. 9.2 Calculate what is necessary for you to meet your quota. 9.3 Create a list of "to-dos," with timelines. 9.4 Plan an agenda for a meeting with your supervisor to review and amend your plan. 9.5 Monitor and update the action plan as necessary, to ensure you stay on track.	The original objective implied that salespeople would be responsible for setting their own sales goals. This is not the case. Salespeople need to understand the sales quota requirements, and create a plan to meet (or exceed) those requirements. The new objective addresses this need, and incorporates working with managers to assist and guide.

Participants will use templates provided in the participant guide, but will be encouraged to customize as much as they like. It will be up to their individual managers to provide feedback on, and monitor the implementation of, the action plan.

Impact on Participants. The participants will have insight into the expectations of a typical sales manager. They will understand the types of goals and achievements a sales manager looks for and be able to create an action plan to use as the basis for a conversation with their own sales manager, as well as to direct their early on-the-job performance.

Impact on Design. Designers will need to create action plan worksheets and provide compensation calculations (handout) to the participants.

Impact on Facilitation Team. The facilitation team will assist by coaching the guest speaker(s) to ensure that they reinforce what is taught in the training class and to keep their comments of a generic nature, so that each individual participant is sufficiently prepared for what to expect back in his or her own field office. In addition, the facilitators will circulate throughout the room while the new hires are completing their action plans.

Impact on the Organization. This process will ultimately assist the organization because it is teaching self-sufficiency to the new hire salespeople. When they understand and embrace the idea that setting sales goals, and the steps required to achieve the sales goals, will ultimately be their own responsibility, they are more likely to perform the process diligently rather than wait for instructions from their sales manager.

Impact on the Job. Action planning should not end when the training program is over. Participants will be encouraged to continuously adapt and update the action plan, and eventually create a customized format that they will use on a regular basis.

Assessment Plan. Ultimately each sales manager will assess whether or not the action plan is sufficient for success in his or her sales office. Each sales manager will undoubtedly have more information about what is truly achievable in his or her territory.

CLIENT DELIVERABLE: REDESIGNED CLASSROOM-BASED TRAINING AGENDA

Based on the work done honing and defining both the learning objectives and impacts on various stakeholders, classroom training for new sales hires for ABC Company is now the clearly focused program described in Tables 4-10 and 4-11. As you progress through the upcoming chapters on different delivery methodologies, you will see a strong connection to the work we have done here. The learning objectives will not change as different delivery mediums are considered. Instead, the learning objectives will become the design foundation for the team as it moves forward to consider asynchronous, synchronous, and blended learning options.

CONCLUSION

In the next chapter, you'll learn how to develop effective asynchronous training based on the fully validated learning objectives presented in this chapter. As you will see, successful blending of learning solutions begins with the carefully developed roadmap we have constructed over the last four chapters.

Table 4-10. Day 1

Timing	Topic	Objective	Materials Needed	Process/Activity	Potential for Assessment	Comments
8:00–8:15	Housekeeping Welcome					
8:15–8:45	Student Introductions (Note: This process will be repeated throughout the day until all participants have introduced themselves.)	1. Represent the organi-zation in a professional manner.	Instructions to participants in advance of session	Each individual has five minutes to speak; are critiqued using feedback form.	Fellow participants will assess using feedback form.	
8:45–11:15 (includes 15-minute break)	Product Knowledge Basics	2. Describe the features and benefits of the company's five core products to prospective buyers.	Workbook	Lecture: 10 minutes per product 10-minute "quiz" after lecture 30-minute "field trip" 20-minute small group activity: matching client "scenario" to best product 10-minute debrief		

(continued on page 80)

Table 4-10. Day 1 (continued)

Timing	Topic	Objective	Materials Needed	Process/Activity	Potential for Assessment	Comments
11:15–11:45	Student Introductions	(1)				
11:45–12:45	Selling Against the Competition	3. Compare and contrast the company's core products with the products of our three closest competitors.		Independent research: 20 minutes Small group activity: 10 minutes Presentation: five minutes each group		
12:45–1:30			LUNCH			
1:30–2:00	Student Introductions	(1)				
2:00–3:00	Prospecting	4. Target high-potential prospects.	Prospecting tool Prospect profile handout	20-minute lecture 20-minute activity 20-minute debrief		
3:00–3:15	Break					
3:15–3:45	Student Introductions	(1)				

3:45–5:00	Open a Sales Call	5. Demonstrate the ability to open a sales call.	Video Workbook Role-play instructions/ handout	20-minute video 30-minute role play 2 minutes brainstorming on questions
5:00–5:30	End of Day 1 Wrap Up			Each salesperson will share a key learning for the day.

Note: All student introductions should be completed by the end of Day 1.

Table 4-11. Day 2

Timing	Topic	Objective	Materials Needed	Process/Activity	Potential for Assessment	Comments
8:00–8:15	Review of Day 1 Q&A					
8:15–9:15	Manage a Meeting	6. Demonstrate the ability to manage a prospect meeting.	Completed Profiling and Qualifying Tools Triad instructions	15-minute lecture and exercise setup 10-minute group activity 35-minute group presentation and debrief		
9:15–11:15	Close a Call	7. Demonstrate the ability to close a sales call.	Video Role-play instructions	30-minute video 60-minute role play 20-minute debrief 10-minute break (where appropriate)		
11:15–12:15	Objections	8. Manage objections.	Instructions for objections game	Four teams will create four to five common objections in one "category" (given to them). Then each team will "pitch" them to the three other teams, who will respond in a way that will keep the conversation with the prospect going.		

Time					
12:15–1:00	LUNCH				
1:00–3:00	Setting Sales Goals	9. Implement an action plan designed to meet quota in the specified time period.	Action planning worksheet	Guest speaker (sales manager) Independent activity	
3:00–3:15	BREAK				
3:15–3:45	End of Day 2 Wrap Up			Each salesperson will share a personal challenge they need to overcome to ensure personal success.	
3:45	Dismissal to get ready for 5:00 p.m. group dinner and "graduation photo"				

Chapter 5

Asynchronous Learning— Make It Interactive and Engaging

The design presented in chapter 4 assumed the training would be delivered entirely in a classroom format. The design presented in this chapter takes the opposite approach—no live training with an instructor during the learning process. However, the facilitators will check in with the new hires periodically to ensure they are progressing through the training and to answer any questions. This asynchronous approach will begin to illustrate the focus on achieving objectives rather than concentrating on the learning methodology.

WHAT IS ASYNCHRONOUS LEARNING?

Back in chapter 1, asynchronous learning was defined as learning that is completed independently and conducted at one's own pace; it is not constrained by geography or time. There are numerous approaches to delivering training in an asynchronous way. Asynchronous learning can be paper based, such as teaching yourself to use Excel by studying *Excel for Dummies*. It may be Internet based, by using email and discussion boards—the University of Phoenix has perfected this model. Or it could be e-learning, which encompasses many technology-based options, such as a "how-to" course accessed via the web, a computer simulation distributed via CD-ROM, or even something as simple as a PowerPoint file with embedded narrations. The difference lies in the level of interaction desired, the level of assessment required, and how much money an organization has to spend (see Figure 5-1).

One of the key benefits of asynchronous e-learning is its convenience. Participants can complete their training when and where they want, so long as they have access to the appropriate technology. Information can be processed at a pace that is appropriate for the individual, and participants can access the information for review as many times as they feel is necessary. Learning can be disseminated to large groups of individuals simultaneously, and updates to content are usually easy to implement.

Asynchronous e-learning has disadvantages as well:

- Because the trainee is left to learn on his or her own, the course design requires a participant who is particularly self-directed and self-motivated. Without specific deadlines and deliverables, it is often hard for participants to put training at the top of their priority list.

Figure 5–1. Asynchronous Training Options

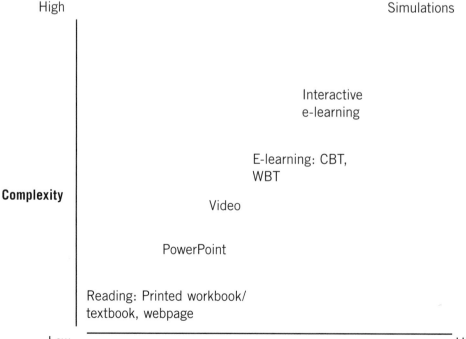

- A course may take days or weeks to complete, depending on the amount of time the employee has to dedicate to it. When the learning process is choppy, the trainee can end up grasping nothing.
- Support is often lacking. If a participant has trouble understanding a piece of content, whom does he or she contact for help? If there are enough unanswered questions, a participant often will give up and move on to "real work."
- A topic that requires interpersonal interaction (such as negotiation skills or counseling skills) can be difficult to translate to an asynchronous environment. Asynchronous training is best suited to the transfer of knowledge, and sales skills are largely interpersonal skills.
- One of the greatest disadvantages of asynchronous learning is that it is often much more expensive to develop than other methods of training (see sidebar "Development Time for Delivery Methods").

Finally, it is a sad fact that most asynchronous learning is boring. Listening, reading, or watching hours of content does not guarantee learning; so attention must be given to creating active and interactive asynchronous learning experiences.

THE ASYNCHRONOUS TRAINING DESIGN AT ABC COMPANY

Designing a program in an asynchronous format is very different from classroom delivery. What was once a two-day, facilitator-led program will now be

---

Development Time for Delivery Methods

According to *The ASTD Media Selection Tool for Workplace Learning* (1999), development time per individual delivery method breaks down as follows:

- **Traditional classroom training:** Forty hours of development for one hour of instruction.
- **Computer-based training:** Two hundred hours of development for one hour of instruction.
- **Video-based training:** Forty to 120 hours of development for one hour of instruction.
- **Web/Internet-based training:** Development times cited for other mediums are similar for delivery over the Internet.

stretched out over a much longer period of time and will be interspersed with on-the-job activities.

The asynchronous approach is advantageous to ABC Company because a new hire could begin his or her training at anytime. However, to allow new hires to start their training at the time they join the organization would require the facilitators to monitor many individuals and their progress, which would prove to be cumbersome, if not impossible. Therefore, it will be recommended that ABC Company begin small groups of new hires (20 or less) in the training process simultaneously. Because of the camaraderie of the group experience, this approach also will result in a richer dialogue occurring in the discussion board and wiki environments, as participants will be eager to deepen their relationships. (For more information on using discussion boards and wikis at ABC Company, see chapter 8.)

An advantage of this approach is that the proposed design and supporting technologies are inexpensive and relatively easy to maintain. No new resource (for example, media specialists, instructional technologist) needs to be engaged to ensure the implementation actually works.

The Role of the Facilitator

While there are many advantages to using an asynchronous approach to training new hires, the design team has some concerns about the participants feeling disconnected, and ABC Company management is concerned about the participants not doing the work without some sort of oversight. While the nature of asynchronous training is independent learning, ABC Company wants a facilitator to stay involved. The new hires are relatively young and have not had the opportunity to be self-directed participants; therefore, ABC Company wants to have someone coach them through the learning process.

To manage these concerns, a discussion board will be implemented and moderated by the facilitators. New hires will be required to contribute to a daily "Training Diary" throughout their training period. Questions will be posted by the facilitator, and responses will be moderated. Questions will fall into two categories: (1) questions specific to the content, which will help to ensure completion and understanding; and (2) questions about the sales training experience, to assist participants who may be struggling with independent learning or support within their field office. A wiki will be created to allow participants to post questions and connect with peers. The sales manager should have a very active role in this learning process, as well as some flexibility as to how the learning is implemented.

The sales manager's role is to direct the learning; the facilitator's role is to ensure that participants complete assignments and that they get sufficient support from their sales office to ensure success.

Schedule

The asynchronous components of this curriculum will be completed over the course of two weeks, as compared with the two-day classroom-based offering. The schedule (see Table 5-10 at the end of this chapter) will allow the new hire sales training content to be augmented with on-the-job activities that will help to reinforce, or better teach, the concepts. The schedule does not fill a new hire's day for the entire two-week period. The unallocated time will be spent on completing structured activities such as learning how to use the Customer Relationship Management system (using tutorials from the vendor); reviewing and contributing to the sales training wikis and blogs; and meeting with the office administrator to learn how to utilize office resources such as email, proposal templates, and sales tracking software.

The biggest advantage for ABC Company in implementing this extended format is that new hire salespeople can learn in less intensive chunks of information, and start to practice skills in their actual workplace prior to moving on to new content. Retention should go up, and participants will have access to the content whenever they need it, for review purposes, after the training is complete.

NEWLY DESIGNED OBJECTIVES AND DESIGN CONSIDERATIONS

As in the previous chapter, the asynchronous design will look at each individual objective and propose a learning approach that best achieves that objective. In some cases, the approach(es) will be very similar, and in other cases, quite different.

Objective 1

Table 5-1 illustrates Objective 1: Represent the organization in a professional manner.

Asynchronous Design Approach. This objective will be addressed in four different ways. The content for Objective 1.1 (Define professionalism) will be presented via a short online video of the president of ABC Company talking about its history and reputation and the importance for all new hires to uphold that reputation through their dress, speech, and interactions with clients and

Table 5-1. Represent the Organization in a Professional Manner

Old Objective	New Objective	Rationale
See new objective.	1. Represent the organization in a professional manner. 1.1 Define professionalism. 1.2 Select attire that conforms to company guidelines. 1.3 Develop rapport. 1.4 Utilize body language and eye contact in a way that creates a comfortable environment.	This objective was culled from the old objective, which stated: "Demonstrate the ability to open a sales call and *behave in a professional manner.*" This objective was created as a stand-alone objective because behaving in a professional manner should be a core skill regardless of what task an individual is performing. The organization considers this an important objective to call out and practice because the majority of new hires come directly from college and have limited professional experience.

in the community at large. Objective 1.2 (Select attire that conforms to company guidelines) will have employees refer to their employee handbook (which they should have just recently received and read) and submit a sign-off sheet that indicates that they have read the parameters for proper attire. Objective 1.3 (Develop rapport) will be addressed via a short reading assignment from *The Sales Bible: The Ultimate Sales Resource* (Jeffrey Gitomer, 2008), either online or in PDF format, explaining the value of salespeople developing rapport with their prospects and clientele.

Objective 1.4 (Utilize body language and eye contact in a way that creates a comfortable environment) is an interpersonal skill that requires practice; therefore, it will be addressed at the very end of the curriculum to allow the participants to have practice interacting with their peers, managers, and potential clients. The culminating activity for this sub-objective, after all training has been completed, will be to schedule and make a presentation to their fellow, more experienced, salespeople in their field offices. The presentations will wrap up all of the presentation-oriented objectives, and will allow colleagues to quiz them on product knowledge and sales situations.

To practice for this portion of the presentation, participants will be given a tip sheet that provides advice on things like shaking hands, maintaining good posture, and maintaining appropriate distance and eye contact (see sidebar "Body Language and Eye Contact Tip Sheet"). This will be accompanied by a short evaluation form that participants can use to assess people they speak with during the course of the training. The intent of this form is to help participants understand how others come across as professional (or unprofessional) based on their body language. This same evaluation form will be used during *their* final presentation as part of their own personal assessment.

Body Language and Eye Contact Tip Sheet

When speaking with prospects or making a presentation, keep these tips in mind.

Body Language

DO:
- ❏ Give firm handshake at beginning and end of meeting.
- ❏ Keep hands in a natural position by your side.

DON'T:
- ❏ Cross your arms.
- ❏ Drum your fingers.
- ❏ Fidget with things in your pocket (change, keys).
- ❏ Slouch in your chair.
- ❏ Pace.

Eye Contact

DO:
- ❏ Make direct eye contact anytime you begin to speak—then you may look away.
- ❏ When making a presentation be sure to make eye contact with everyone in attendance at least once.
- ❏ When making a presentation, scan the group as you speak.

DON'T:
- ❏ Look at the floor.
- ❏ Look "above" or "beyond" the other individual(s).
- ❏ Squint.

Impact on Participants. This objective may present a challenge for new hires because there are a number of sub-objectives, each treated via a different learning approach, which might prove confusing. Participants also may feel at a loss as to what to do with their time (because the training schedule does not fill an entire day), or feel as if they are not being truly welcomed by the company because they are left to learn "on their own." These feelings can be mitigated by interaction with the facilitator and sales manager (or mentor) during their first two or three days of training.

Impact on Design. This design approach is also challenging for the designers of the training. The participants need to be fully apprised of how to access each element of the asynchronous training (videos, online modules) to be successful, and that may prove difficult for designers to accomplish in an asynchronous manner. The asynchronous training program will require a participant manual with a syllabus that outlines for the participant, perhaps on a daily basis, the following: 1) what element or objective(s) should be learned; and 2) very clear instructions regarding how that particular piece of content is accessed. A video of the president's message and the Body Language and Eye Contact Tip Sheet also will need to be created.

Impact on Facilitation Team. The facilitation team should be in contact with participants as soon as they are hired, so new hires have a point of contact and understand they have an advocate who is concerned with their success in the new hire training program. The facilitator(s) will send out the training materials with a cover note explaining the training process and the facilitator's role in supporting the new hire participant. Because it is possible for more than 20 people to go through the asynchronous training process at a time, more facilitators may be required to keep the facilitator-to-participant ratio at a level that allows the facilitator to develop a supportive relationship with each trainee. This can be evaluated after the first few groups of participants complete the process under the 20-or-less attendees parameter discussed earlier. The facilitation team will be responsible for keeping the participants on track with the training schedule and connected with one another by utilizing the wiki and discussion board.

Impact on the Organization. An asynchronous approach to new hire orientation and training is dangerous in that the new hire may feel abandoned immediately upon joining the company. Every effort needs to be made to communicate to the participants the value of the asynchronous training approach—from the participants' perspective—such as being able to take the training at their own pace; the ability to review any content they feel they did not master; and the ability to contact their facilitator with any questions they have about the training process or the content they have learned.

Impact on the Job. The asynchronous training approach means that participants can access the training from their own individual sales offices. This in turn means that the participants can actually get started in their jobs faster by supplementing training modules with on-the-job experiences with their manager or a more seasoned salesperson (mentor). In addition, the electronic resources will continue to be available after the official training is over—so they can be used as a resource in the future.

Assessment Plan. The culminating activity for participants, after all training has been completed, will be to schedule and make a presentation to the more seasoned salespeople in their field offices. The presentation to their colleagues will demonstrate, in accordance with the fulfillment of Objective 1, their understanding of professional dress, their skill at rapport-building, and their ability to utilize effective eye contact and body language.

Objective 2

Table 5-2 illustrates Objective 2: Describe the features and benefits of the company's five core products to prospective buyers.

Table 5-2. Describe the Features and Benefits of the Company's Five Core Products to Prospective Buyers

Old Objective	New Objective	Rationale
Describe our basic product offering.	2. Describe the features and benefits of the company's five core products to prospective buyers. 2.1 What are the core products of each? 2.2 What are the features and benefits? 2.3 Identify which product most closely aligns with a prospect's needs.	The original objective was vague, and not complete. What do we mean by "describe"? To whom? What should be included? Does each prospect receive the same description? Also, the phrase "basic product offering" was left to interpretation. The company carries more than 30 products—which are to be considered "basic"? The new objective addresses these questions.

Asynchronous Design Approach. This topic will be accessible via an online slideshow (for example, PowerPoint) and supported by a workbook. The slideshow will provide static pictures of each of the five core products and use callouts or hotspots to describe the features and benefits of each. The workbook will allow participants to take additional notes about each of the products, and can be used as a reference tool in the early stages of their sales career as they are becoming more familiar with the products. The workbook will contain information on *all* of the company's products, not just the five core products required for this objective; so it will be a one-stop resource. The workbook will have pocket sleeves that allow the participant to insert the marketing materials that are associated with each product; in this way he or she will be able to keep the basic product information and the sales-oriented information that a prospect will receive all in one place. A summative page in the workbook will feature a chart that identifies common client needs or uses, and the product(s) that can fulfill those needs and uses (see sidebar "Sample Workbook Page").

Impact on Participants. The participants should find this activity engaging and interactive because they will be able to manipulate the pictures and the text on screen. The format also will be quite helpful because they will be able to review it as many times as necessary until they have internalized the information. Once the activity is completed, the workbook will act as a stand-alone reference, combining corporate information and personal observations. When not involved in formal learning, the participants can use some of their non-allocated time to collect the requisite marketing materials and review them.

Impact on Design. This is a very straightforward design, especially because the creation of the online product descriptions can simply be re-purposed for the printed workbook. Using PowerPoint to create the content allows the information to be updated easily by almost anyone in the organization.

Impact on Facilitation Team. The facilitation team should have no role in this learning objective unless participants have a particular question. However, because the information is so basic and factual, there really should be no questions.

Impact on the Organization. The five core products constitute the content that each participant must master to successfully sell ABC Company's products. This content should not change over the years, as the objective covers only the five core products.

Impact on the Job. The new hire's performance on the job is completely dependent on understanding ABC Company's product offerings and how they differ from one another. The process of locating the marketing materials during the training will familiarize new hires with how to find similar

Sample Workbook Page

ABC Company's Core Products	Notes

While we carry 30 products in total, you will find that our five core products are the best sellers. They are:

(Fill in)

1. _____

2. _____

3. _____

4. _____

5. _____

Each product has one distinct feature that sets it apart from the other four. When you are making a sales call, listen to what the prospect mentions as a need or frustration with his or her current product. Typically, you will hear a need that aligns with one of the features below, and you will know which product to start offering.

Product 1 features high density. . . .

Product 2 features high capacity. . . .

Product 3 features the ability to network with other. . . .

Product 4 features a scalable. . . .

Product 5 features the smallest footprint. . . .

information (later on in their offices) for the 25 products that are not being specifically taught.

Assessment Plan. A drag-and-drop self-assessment will be created in the online version of this training to have participants correctly identify each of the five core products and label the features and benefits associated with each one.

Objective 3

Table 5-3 illustrates Objective 3: Compare and contrast the company's core products with the products of our three closest competitors.

Table 5-3. Compare and Contrast the Company's Core Products With the Products of Our Three Closest Competitors

Old Objective	New Objective	Rationale
Compare and contrast our product and sales platform with our three closest competitors.	3. Compare and contrast the company's core products with the products of our three closest competitors. 3.1 Identify closest competitors, including characteristics that define them as closest competitors. 3.2 Identify competitor offerings that most closely align with our own. 3.3 Compare similarities and contrast differences between the competitor's products and our core products.	The original objective contained jargon ("sales platform") that not even the sales managers could define; so that language was removed. In addition, it is ambitious to assume that new hires can leave the program being able to discuss more than 30 products; so the objective now references the core products, identified in Objective 2.

Asynchronous Design Approach. Very similar to the classroom design approach for this objective, participants will be instructed to use the Internet to research ABC Company's three closest competitors and compare their core products with the ones they learned while completing the requirements for Objective 2. A checklist of items to look for will be provided, so participants know what to focus on while doing their Internet research (see sidebar "Manager's Checklist for New Hire Independent Competitor Research"). The participants will conclude their research with a synopsis of what they have learned, similar to what they might say to a client who asks them to compare and contrast two products; they will then be tasked with making a one-on-one presentation to their sales manager. The sales manager will ask questions, as a prospect might, to gather more information about the products. The sales manager also will correct or augment any information about the competitor's products, as necessary.

Impact on Participants. This is a research and learning process that the participant will be able to use again and again, whenever a competitor introduces a new product. The sales manager will be provided with a list of key points the participant should have identified via the research, so he or she can provide feedback during the presentation. Giving a presentation to the sales manager will provide a realistic practice opportunity.

Impact on Design. A worksheet will be developed so participants have a focus for their Internet research. It will include such things as the number of products carried by the competitor (in total), the number of products that are most closely aligned with ABC's five core products, and how those products are similar or different. An answer key will be developed, in the form of a completed worksheet and sample synopsis, for the sales managers to evaluate the presentation.

Impact on Facilitation Team. The facilitation team will post discussion questions about the competitors during the time the participants are conducting their research. For instance, participants generally conduct competitor research on Day 3 or 4 of their training; so the facilitators will post discussion questions such as: "While it is true all three competitors you are researching offer the same products and services we do, there is only one that targets our client demographic. Which one is it, and how does it compare?"

Impact on the Organization. This process will assist the organization by teaching new salespeople research and comparative analysis skills. It also will help the sales managers identify potential performance issues early in the training process (time management, ability to follow instructions), so they can give appropriate guidance.

Manager's Checklist for New Hire Independent Competitor Research

Competitor 1	Competitor 2	Competitor 3
Product closest to ABC Company's X product is: B	Product closest to ABC Company's Y product is: L	Product closest to ABC Company's Z product is: O
Market niche they target: small	Market niche they target: medium	Market niche they target: large
Product B's: Footprint: 13 x 42 x 13 Output/Throughput: 55 ppm Replaceable parts: oil/lubricant, bearings, cartridges Service package cost: $299 one time Expandability: not compatible with other units, but will allow trade-in to product D as company grows	Product L's: Footprint: 24 x 42 x 36 Output/Throughput: 80 ppm Replaceable parts: oil/lubricant, bearings, cartridges, fuse rods Service package cost: $199 first year; $59 per year after that Expandability: not compatible with other units	Product O's: Footprint: 50 x 100 x 45 Output/Throughput: 250 ppm Replaceable parts: oil/lubricant, bearings, cartridges, fuse rods, air and lubricant gauges; stand needs to be replaced every three years due to wear Service package cost: does not say on website Expandability: can be combined with product P, R, or P *and* R to double or triple throughput—but space for footprint would have to be allowed at first installation (assuming company growth)

Synopsis:

Products X and B are nearly identical; the major difference is the speed of output. If the customer is on the small side (fewer than 500 workers), our product (X) is fine and slightly less expensive. With the added service package, the client could own the product, worry-free for five years, for the same price as Competitor 1's product B. However, if the company is approaching 700 workers, or will in the foreseeable future, product B would be better due to its higher output speed. The customer (organization) would have better efficiency with product B than with ours.

Impact on the Job. A large part of the salesperson's job is to understand ABC Company's product offerings, as well as those of their competitors, so he or she can emphasize the advantage of ABC's offerings. The sales presentation to their managers will help the new hire salespeople master this skill.

Assessment Plan. A two-part written assessment will be created. The first part will be a matching quiz listing the three major competitors in the left column and all their products in the right column. The participant will need to move each product name to the appropriate area of the left column, indicating which company carries that product. The second part of the quiz will show a picture of a competitor's product with three to five features and benefits listed underneath. The participant will need to point to the appropriate spot on the product and label it with the appropriate feature and benefit (see sidebar "Competitor Product Knowledge Assessment"). Finally, the participant will have to write a synopsis about ABC Company's comparable product and how it surpasses that of the competitor. In other words, what would the salesperson tell a prospect to compel him or her to choose ABC Company's product over the competitor's similar product? The assessment will be reviewed by the participants' sales manager and the training facilitator will be copied. The final part of the assessment for Objective 3 is to make the presentation, mentioned earlier, to their sales manager.

Objective 4

Table 5-4 illustrates Objective 4: Target high-potential prospects.

Table 5-4. Target High-Potential Prospects

Old Objective	New Objective	Rationale
Describe the characteristics of a viable prospect.	4. Target high-potential prospects. 4.1 Describe the characteristics of a viable prospect. 4.2 Develop a prioritized prospecting list. 4.3 Create a customized approach to engage the prospect in a sales conversation.	The original objective did not take this concept far enough. A salesperson must do more then describe a viable prospect; he or she must identify prospects and then find a way to engage them.

Competitor Product Knowledge Assessment

PART 1

Match the product names in the right column, with the competitor that sells them, in the left column.

Competitor 1	
_____	
_____	
_____	Product A
_____	Product B
	Product C
Competitor 2	Product D
_____	Product E
_____	Product L
_____	Product M
_____	Product N
	Product O
Competitor 3	Product P
_____	Product R
_____	Produce W
_____	
_____	

PART 2

Using the list of features below the illustration, identify each area of the illustration by pointing an arrow to it and labeling it.

Product O, offered by Competitor 1

Retractable filament   Cooling switch   Power boost switch

Asynchronous Design Approach. Because the information about viable prospects is rather straightforward, this content will be designed in a self-paced, online format that will allow for narration (PowerPoint or a similar tool will be used). Participants will be able to read text about the ideal qualities of a prospect and hear narration that augments what they are reading. The narration becomes particularly beneficial when the Profiling and Qualifying Tool is introduced (see chapter 4). The online format will allow portions of the tool to be displayed individually as the narrator discusses how the tool is used. The tool will identify such things as number of employees, minimum number of locations considered to be ideal in a prospect, and parameters for company earnings. This approach will help the new salespeople understand that not all prospects are viable customers. A hard copy of the tool will be included in the participants' training materials as well, so they can follow along with the online learning.

Impact on Participants. Participants should be able to quickly assimilate the qualifying criteria of a viable prospect and apply those criteria to any sales leads they encounter. The Profiling and Qualifying Tool will be available to participants after the training is completed, so it can be used to support actual prospecting activity.

Impact on Design. The tool has already been created, thanks to one of the facilitators; it may need to be tweaked a bit once the ideal prospect characteristics are vetted with a number of field office managers.

Impact on Facilitation Team. The facilitation team will check in with the participants during this learning objective because understanding that "not all prospects are good prospects" is sometimes a hard concept to grasp. Once participants have completed the online learning module and assessment (see Assessment Plan below), facilitators will call them individually and review the Profiling and Qualifying Tool with them over the phone. The assessment results will help the facilitators know what areas to concentrate their coaching on when speaking with the participant.

Impact on the Organization. Prospecting is a crucial skill to master to maximize a salesperson's time and closing ratios by pursuing only quality leads. Having the participants learn the process and thinking skills in an online format that allows them to review the concept as many times as necessary, combined with the case study assessment and one-on-one coaching from the facilitator, should help to ensure mastery of this topic.

Impact on the Job. While the posttraining quota assigned a new hire salesperson is doable, the past participants who were interviewed during the assessment stage thought the quota expectations were aggressive. Initially, utilizing the Profiling and Qualifying Tool will mean fewer sales for the new hire because they will be required to be more selective when pursuing a prospect.

However, the overall success ratio should be higher for any salesperson using this tool and this process.

Assessment Plan. The assessment will include profiles of 10 prospects and will require the participant to drag and drop the prospect's names, in order, with one being the most viable prospect and 10 being the least viable prospect. Should participants drag a prospect into an incorrect position, a pop-up window will explain the key information they should consider and refer them back to the profile of that prospect. Participants will be allowed two attempts to reposition a prospect, if they had trouble correctly identifying its position. After two attempts, the system will automatically place that prospect in the correct numeric position and allow the participants to continue with the remaining placements.

Objective 5

Table 5-5 illustrates Objective 5: Demonstrate the ability to open a sales call.

Table 5-5. Demonstrate the Ability to Open a Sales Call

Old Objective	New Objective	Rationale

Demonstrate the ability to open a sales call and behave in a professional manner.	5. Demonstrate the ability to open a sales call.
	
	  5.1 Greet the prospect.
	
	  5.2 Propose an agenda for the meeting, state the value to the prospect, and check that the prospect accepts your agenda.
	
	  5.3 Ask questions that uncover the prospect's true need.
		"Behave in a professional manner" was determined to be an independent objective and is now addressed in Objective 1.
		
		The steps involved in opening a sales call are now defined, so that they can be more clearly assessed.

Asynchronous Design Approach. Participants will watch a video with five vignettes of salespeople opening various sales calls with potential clients. At the end of each vignette, a narrator will "lecture" about what the salesperson demonstrated, how it was received by the prospect (client), and why that might be a good initial opening to a sales call. Two to three discussion questions for each vignette will be developed that require participants to prepare an answer and then post their response to the discussion board for feedback by the facilitator.

Once the video-based training, discussion questions, and discussion board postings have been completed, the participant will begin to go on sales calls with a more seasoned salesperson from his or her field office. It would be ideal if the senior salesperson were able to concentrate on prospects for these visits, rather than calling on current clients. As the trainee and the more senior salesperson are driving to each sales call, the senior salesperson will conduct a conversation about the types of questions he or she intends to ask of the prospect and the reasoning behind those questions. Once a sales call is complete, the more senior salesperson will conduct another conversation asking the participant what he or she observed, why he or she thinks the more senior salesperson chose the questions he or she did, or if there were any changes to the intended approach based on the response received from the prospect.

Impact on Participants. Watching various salespeople demonstrate alternative openings to sales calls will help the participant understand that each sales call is unique. The discussion questions will help participants consider different approaches and highlight the need to tailor their initial sales call openings to what they know about their prospect.

Impact on Design. The video will be purchased from a sales training vendor, and the discussion questions will be developed by the design team. Senior salespeople with a passion for growing talent will be chosen from each field office to support new hires as they are brought on. In addition, a set of conversation guidelines will be created for the senior salespeople to ensure they are helping the participant think objectively and critically about each sales call.

Impact on Facilitation Team. The facilitators will monitor the discussion board for participant responses and provide feedback regarding the best approaches to open a sales call. This discussion board posting and monitoring also will allow the facilitators to assess who is falling behind in the training schedule, as each participant should be at this segment of their training at approximately Day 4.

Impact on the Organization. A salesperson who is able to continue a dialogue with a prospect is more likely to get repeat appointments and close a sale within two to three visits. Therefore, it is imperative the new hire salesperson be able to effectively open a sales call and pursue a dialogue with a qualified prospect.

Impact on the Job. This is the first time the participant is able to see his or her role in action by accompanying a senior salesperson on sales calls. This process should help the participant better understand how what he or she has been learning applies on the job.

Assessment Plan. Once the salesperson has been on the job for two to three months, the sales manager should accompany that individual on a number of new prospect sales calls to observe how the new hire conducts the opening, and then pursues questions to obtain more information to further the dialogue with the prospect. The sales manager will use a feedback form to check for certain behaviors, such as asking open-ended questions. He or she will then use that form to provide feedback to the participant. This assessment process will be explained to the participant at the end of the video learning portion of the training.

Objective 6

Table 5-6 illustrates Objective 6: Demonstrate the ability to manage a prospect meeting.

Table 5-6. Demonstrate the Ability to Manage a Prospect Meeting

Old Objective	New Objective	Rationale
See new objective.	6. Demonstrate the ability to manage a prospect meeting. 6.1 Probe for clarification. 6.2 Suggest solutions that meet the need.	This objective was added because, effectively, the course had been teaching salespeople enough to get in the door, but not providing them the skills they needed after they arrived. The new objective attempts to assist salespeople in managing the meeting and working with the prospect to devise a solution that ultimately results in a sale.

Asynchronous Design Approach. The participant workbook will contain a reading assignment about the purpose and construction of open-ended and closed-ended questions and the need to create an agenda or an outline for each sales call. It will refer trainees back to the chart used to teach Objective 2, which aligns a prospect's needs with a particular ABC Company product offering. This exercise also will address the uncovering of a prospect's true need with effective questioning techniques. Following the reading assignment, the participants will rewrite a set of closed-ended questions in an open-ended way. Participants will submit their rewritten questions to the sales training facilitators via e-mail and will receive feedback via a phone call.

Participants will review completed Profiling and Qualifying Tools for two fictitious prospects, and develop an appropriate set of questions to help clarify the prospects' needs. These questions will be posted to the discussion board. The facilitators will act as the prospect and answer the questions, after which each participant will determine the best solution(s) to meet those needs. These solutions, and their justifications, will be posted to the discussion board for feedback from the facilitators and sales managers.

Impact on Participants. The most important element of any sales call is to keep the door open; participants will learn to create ongoing conversations with their prospects through the use of planning and questioning.

Impact on Design. This is a very straightforward design, with reading assignments and discussion questions in the workbook.

Impact on Facilitation Team. The facilitators need to monitor each participant they are coaching to ensure the participant is on track to complete this assignment within the timeframe expected. The phone call, which will help to critique and further explain the importance of an open-ended question, can also be used to ask the participants about their experience going on sales calls with the more seasoned salesperson(s) in their office. This process will allow the facilitators to monitor the commitment and performance of the office salespeople who have been chosen to assist during training.

Impact on the Organization. The organization will have a more capable salesforce, which understands more completely the nature of the sales process.

Impact on the Job. Questioning skills are a crucial element of salesperson success. Understanding how to formulate appropriate questions is essential for the participant to be successful on the job.

Assessment Plan. Following the reading assignment and practice of rewriting questions, and the conversation with the training facilitator, participants will refer back to the profiles used in Objective 4 and will be tasked with writing an agenda, as well as constructing two to five questions they might use during their first sales call to gather more information from the prospect.

The agenda and questions will be posted to the discussion board for critique by the training facilitators and fellow training participants.

Objective 7

Table 5-7 illustrates Objective 7: Demonstrate the ability to close a sales call.

Table 5-7. Demonstrate the Ability to Close a Sales Call

Old Objective	New Objective	Rationale
See new objective.	7. Demonstrate the ability to close a sales call. 7.1 Confirm that the meeting has met the prospect's expectation. 7.2 Close the call with suggested next steps and timelines.	This new objective is included to ensure a salesperson can effectively close a sales call. This was not addressed in the original training.

Asynchronous Design Approach. A video of sales closing vignettes will be used to demonstrate closing a sales call. Each vignette will be debriefed by a narrator who will interpret the language of the prospect and point out the cues that indicate the prospect is ready to close the sale. Key to the closing process, and therefore key in the videos, is the salesperson's statement(s) that closes the sale; for instance, "Let's fill out the paperwork then!" or "I'm pleased we will be working together." A job aid or "cheat sheet" will now be introduced that summarizes the steps of the sales process: opening the call, questions that keep the dialogue going, and statements or questions that close a sale. This is something that participants will be instructed to use as a reference tool once they are making their own sales calls; they will be expected to review this job aid to remind themselves of the critical steps prior to any prospect meeting.

Impact on Participants. Often a sale is lost because the salesperson simply does not ask for the sale. It is important to hear the types of statements or questions that are used to close a sale because they don't come naturally in most cases, especially to someone who is new to sales. The video examples and job aid will help participants bring a sales call to a close, with a sale, by giving them appropriate verbiage.

Impact on Design. The video will be purchased off the shelf from a vendor, and the quiz and job aid will be developed in-house to be included in the workbook.

Impact on Facilitation Team. The facilitation team has no role supporting this objective.

Impact on the Organization. Participants will not be expected to master closing a sales call until they have been on the job for three months or more. This is a skill the sales manager may need to revisit with participants, in more of a coaching role, once they have had some time to practice their other skills on the job.

Impact on the Job. Because closing a sale can take place anywhere from three weeks to three months after an initial sales call, the salespeople may have forgotten the closing skills they learned during the training. It is hard to master a skill when it is not used immediately. Therefore, the job aid will assist the new salesperson in remembering the steps of the closing, and the sales manager's coaching should help each participant master the closing process once he or she is on the job.

Assessment Plan. Participants will take a simple quiz in their workbook that lists a number of potential closing statements and asks the participant to check those that would appropriately close a sale. More extensive assessments really cannot be done until participants have had the opportunity to practice making sales calls and getting to the closing process; so a more thorough assessment will be created for three or four months hence.

Objective 8

Table 5-8 illustrates Objective 8: Manage objections.

Table 5-8. Manage Objections

Old Objective	New Objective	Rationale
Respond to objections in an appropriate manner.	8. Manage objections. 8.1 Identify an objection. 8.2 Categorize the objection. 8.3 Respond to the objection in a way that keeps the conversation moving forward.	This objective was reworded to align with Objectives 6 and 7.

Asynchronous Design Approach. An online learning module will teach participants the basic categories of objections and remind them to use probing questions to uncover a real or underlying objection—not simply accept the objection as it is first presented by the prospect. Once participants have a basic understanding of participant objections, they will play an online game that requires them to identify and categorize various objections that might be heard on the job. They will then be tasked with polling all of the salespeople in their office and asking them for the toughest objection they ever encountered. From the collection of responses, participants will choose what they believe is the hardest objection and post it to the discussion board to get other trainees' feedback. They also will be required to respond to the objections posted there by fellow participants throughout the country who are taking the same training simultaneously.

Impact on Participants. The participants will have a basic understanding of the categories in which objections fall as well as be able to identify the root of an objection and respond appropriately, given the underlying objection (for example, timing, budget, and authority). By polling their fellow salespeople in the field office, they will begin to develop relationships and call on the more senior salespeople for assistance, knowing that they, too, faced tough objections when they first started selling. By interacting with their peers (who are also in training) via the discussion board, they will be exposed to a variety of possible objections and will learn to rely upon and assist their peers when they encounter sales challenges in the future.

Impact on Design. An online learning module will need to be developed, and the rest of the learning content will be generated by each sales office and the participant's peers via the discussion board.

Impact on Facilitation Team. The facilitators will monitor the objections that are posted on the discussion board and offer tips for responses as necessary. At this point in the training process, the facilitators should not be seen as the "answer people." They should facilitate the discussion board in a way that helps the participants begin to rely on one another as a resource in their career.

Impact on the Organization. Having salespeople who are confident in knowing that an objection does not mean "no" will lead to increased sales, because these salespeople will continue longer in the sales process than those who hear their first objection and, at that point, end the sales call.

Impact on the Job. As a result of this training process, ABC Company's new hire salespeople will have better success at closing sales because they will understand that an objection is a natural part of the selling process, and they will be appropriately prepared to respond to objections of various types.

They also will be more likely to rely on fellow salespeople in their field office as well as their colleagues across the country when they are faced with a particularly hard objection, because the training process fostered that cooperative relationship.

Assessment Plan. Assessing the participants' success at recognizing and categorizing objections will be done during the learning process (the online activity); however, being able to respond appropriately to an objection in a static environment is entirely different from being faced with an actual objection during the sales process. The true measure of success will be determined by the number of sales each salesperson is able to close as well as how quickly the sales process is closed once the new hire is on the job.

Objective 9

Table 5-9 illustrates Objective 9: Implement an action plan designed to meet quota in the specified time period.

Table 5-9. Implement an Action Plan Designed to Meet Quota in the Specified Time Period

Old Objective	New Objective	Rationale
Set sales goals for self that align with quotas and sales manager expectations.	9. Implement an action plan designed to meet quota in the specified time period. 9.1 Articulate quota requirements. 9.2 Calculate what is necessary for you to meet your quota. 9.3 Create a list of "to-dos," with timelines. 9.4 Plan an agenda for a meeting with your supervisor to review and amend your plan. 9.5 Monitor and update the action plan as necessary, to ensure you stay on track.	The original objective implied that salespeople would be responsible for setting their own sales goals. This is not the case. Salespeople need to understand the sales quota requirements, and create a plan to meet (or exceed) those requirements. The new objective addresses this need, and incorporates working with managers to assist and guide.

Asynchronous Design Approach. Given a template that will include a time-line or organizer, each participant will have a one-on-one meeting with his or her sales manager to set appropriate interim goals during their first three months on the job. While the overall quota of four sales in six months is not negotiable, interim goals for reaching quota can differ from sales manager to sales manager.

Impact on Participants. Participants will have a better expectation of how their particular sales manager will assess, monitor, and support their performance.

Impact on Design. A fill-in-the-blank goal-setting template will need to be created for this portion of the learning process.

Impact on Facilitation Team. The facilitators will check in with each participant during this last objective, to answer any outstanding questions the participant has and also to ensure that the sales manager has taken the time to speak with him or her and shape the first three months of on-the-job experience for each participant.

Impact on the Organization. New hire salespeople should be more successful, earlier in their careers, as a result of the training process occurring in the sales office. This on-the-job coaching gives participants the chance to experience sales calls, understand how a sales office operates, and develop a relationship with their manager much sooner than if they had attended a training class at the corporate headquarters.

Impact on the Job. Participants should have more success earlier in their sales career, and should be able to reach their six-month sales quota more easily. New hires also should see their sales manager as a resource in assisting them to achieve their quota and becoming a successful salesperson within that manager's field office.

Assessment Plan. Ultimately the assessment of goal setting and action planning will be whether or not more of these new hires achieve their sales goal than others have in the past.

DELIVERABLE TO CLIENT

The training agenda found in Table 5-10 outlines the asynchronous training process and the tools needed to achieve success via this training delivery method. Our discussion with the client will note that an asynchronous approach is highly feasible, and that we believe it will successfully achieve the learning goals and business goals of the organization.

Table 5-10. Welcome to ABC Company New Hire Sales Training!

During the course of the next three weeks, you will complete your training in a variety of ways, while your colleagues across the country are completing their training as well. You will find a general outline for your progress below. You will be able to stay in touch with your facilitators [name] [name] and your fellow participants via our discussion board community.

If you encounter any problems, or have any questions about your training, please don't hesitate to contact your facilitators [insert contact information].

Daily Activities	Time Required	Resources Required
Week 1		
Day 1 1. Watch welcome video from president of ABC Company. 2. Read Section 6 of the employee handbook regarding dress code and appropriate office behavior; sign off on page 22 and fax copies to the HR department and training facilitator. 3. Read chapter 12 in *The Sales Bible* regarding rapport building. 4. Review the online learning module that covers ABC Company's core products. 5. Review the common client needs and the ABC Company product alignment chart found in workbook.	Three hours	Video VCR or DVD player Employee handbook Fax machine *The Sales Bible* Access to online learning module New hire training workbook
Day 2 1. Review items four and five from Day 1. 2. Research ABC Company's three closest competitors.	Three hours	Access to online learning module Internet research checklist New hire training workbook

(continued on page 112)

Table 5-10. Welcome to ABC Company New Hire Sales Training! (continued)

Daily Activities	Time Required	Resources Required
3. Write synopsis of what research revealed and make presentation to sales manager.		Features and benefits assessment Access to sales manager
Day 3 1. Review items four and five from Day 1. 2. Review characteristics of a viable prospect and assessment via online learning module.	Three hours	Access to online learning module(s) Profiling and Qualifying Tool New hire training workbook Facilitator check-in
Day 4 1. Review items four and five from Day 1. 2. Watch opening a sales call video. 3. Talk about discussion questions for each video vignette with a senior salesperson in your office or your sales manager.	Three to four hours	Access to online learning module Opening a sales call video VCR or DVD player Senior salesperson or coach identified
Day 5 1. Review items four and five from Day 1. 2. Accompany senior salesperson on sales calls.	Full day	Access to online learning module Conversation guidelines for prospecting calls (provide to a senior salesperson or coach)

Daily Activities	Time Required	Resources Required
Week 2		
Day 6 1. Read workbook pages regarding open-ended and closed-ended questions. 2. Complete closed-ended question activity found in workbook. 3. Submit activity results to training facilitator. 4. Discuss activity results with training facilitator. 5. After discussion with training facilitator, complete client profile activities found in workbook.	Four to five hours	New hire training workbook
Day 7 1. Review items four and five from Day 1. 2. Watch sales closing vignettes video. 3. Review the job aid for the sales process. 4. Check in with sales manager.	Three hours	Access to online learning module Closing a sales call video Job aid summarizing the steps of the sales process Sales manager reviews training progress to date; job aid and completed closing the sale assessment found in participant workbook

(continued on page 114)

Table 5-10. Welcome to ABC Company New Hire Sales Training! (continued)

Daily Activities	Time Required	Resources Required
Day 8 1. Review online learning module for objections. 2. Complete online objections assessment. 3. Poll senior salespeople in your office regarding their toughest objection. 4. Post objections to discussion board and respond to objections posted by other participants.	Four hours	Access to online learning module Access to senior salespeople Access to discussion board
Day 9 1. Complete sales goals action plan with sales manager. 2. Accompany senior salesperson on sales calls.	Full day	Action planning template Access to sales manager
Day 10 Prepare for next week's presentation.	Full day	Access to all learning resources, senior salesperson or coach, sales manager

Week 3

Presentation

You will prepare a presentation to your sales office summarizing the top three things you have learned (from experiences, sales calls, conversations with more senior salespeople, your training facilitator, your manager, and your peers), and demonstrating your presentation skills encompassing eye contact, appropriate body language, and questioning skills. Your fellow salespeople will evaluate you on your knowledge of ABC Company products, your presentation abilities, and your ability to respond to questions or objections.

An evaluation form will be completed, and collected by your sales manager, to provide you feedback in the following areas: presentation skills, product knowledge, and handling objections. Your sales manager may require you to give this presentation again if you do not meet minimum requirements. Once the presentation is complete, you are considered a full-fledged member of your sales office, and your six-month timeframe to meet your quota goal begins.

Congratulations and good luck!

CONCLUSION

You have probably realized that different approaches have been used in this chapter to achieve our "standardized" learning objectives. The key to blended learning is aligning the objective with the *best* delivery approach; so in the next chapter, which analyzes a synchronous approach, you will see a few different designs, yet again. Chapter 7 will finally reveal the best use of each training methodology in alignment with the individual objectives.

—

Chapter 6

Synchronous Learning— Gee, This Was Just Like a Real Class!

Synchronous learning refers to instruction that is led by a facilitator, in real time, using technology. Synchronous interactions include conference calls, instant messaging, video conferences, and virtual classrooms. Typically, the learning methodology is characterized by technology-facilitated group interactions and collaboration among participants, along with discussions or other learning activities. This chapter will discuss the benefits and drawbacks of using synchronous technology as a delivery medium. The discussion of synchronous learning centers on the nine learning objectives established in chapter 4. These objectives remain the roadmap to training development that meets both learning and organizational goals, no matter how it is delivered.

WHY UTILIZE A VIRTUAL CLASSROOM?

The ability to interact with experts and peers in real time is a comfortable and familiar environment and eliminates the isolation that often comes with asynchronous technologies. Often a participant requires live interaction with an instructor or an expert, but that interaction does not need to be face-to-face.

For example, medical students observing surgery would, arguably, benefit from being physically in the operating room or a surgical observation area. However, those same participants do not need face-to-face interaction to ask post-operative questions of the surgeon. Questions can be asked and discussed among all of the participants via a virtual classroom. If a recording is made of the synchronous discussion, all of the participants can go back and review the recording, at any time, to ensure they understood the answers. One of the most common reasons for organizations to implement a virtual classroom is an audience that is dispersed across a large geographic area (oftentimes worldwide). Compared with traditional classroom delivery, the money saved in classroom costs, travel, and time away from work quickly becomes apparent. In addition, organizations may choose to deliver content that they never would have scheduled in a more traditional (classroom) setting. For example, an update to a computer system may take only one or two hours to teach, but an organization would rarely convene a training program for such a short period of time because it would be cost prohibitive. The virtual classroom makes this type of content easy to distribute.

As organizations become more global, and the need to collaborate across a distance is becoming more important, a virtual meeting place can help close the distance gap by providing a forum through which employees collaborate in real time. (See chapter 8 for a discussion of collaboration tools that can be used in a self-directed format.)

While the benefits of using a virtual classroom are many, there are some drawbacks as well. The most obvious is the ease of use in regard to technologies. If a trainee cannot participate successfully from the onset, because the technology is a barrier, a negative impression of the training itself can develop. Even when the technology works seamlessly, it is difficult for some participants and facilitators alike to believe that the virtual classroom can ever be as effective as a more traditional classroom format simply because of its distributed nature. Another issue is the length of classes. Best practices dictate that a synchronous session be between 60 and 120 minutes in length; so eight hours of content would require four, two-hour modules. Organizations are concerned about attendance and participation, and do not see a series of sessions to be reasonable.

Perhaps one of the most persuasive arguments that participants have against learning in a virtual classroom is their own past experience. Years of hourlong content dumps and subject matter expert presentations have convinced audiences that the virtual classroom is not conducive to true learning; it is simply a way to get information. All of these negative perceptions can be overcome via a quality design and delivery process. A virtual class is often considered the best of both worlds—synchronous (instructor led) and asynchronous (independent)—because the most effective design encompasses elements of each, as you will see in this chapter.

THE SYNCHRONOUS TRAINING DESIGN

When considering the asynchronous approach, ABC Company's primary concern was ensuring that participants completed the self-directed work. In the synchronous format, the concern is the potential for participants to multitask or be distracted. To create a successful training plan, the synchronous approach is interspersed with asynchronous modules and on-the-job practice activities. Figure 6-1 is an example of a page from a synchronous leader guide, which indicates how participants will learn from one another in a synchronous classroom. Notice the distinction between the facilitator's role and the producer's role.

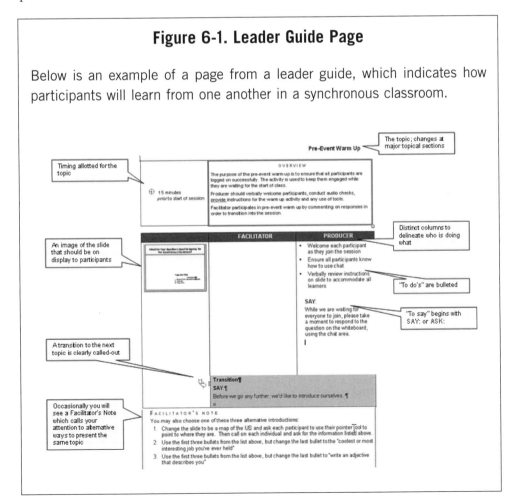

Figure 6-1. Leader Guide Page

Below is an example of a page from a leader guide, which indicates how participants will learn from one another in a synchronous classroom.

The training design will assume that both facilitators will continue to be present at all live sessions. One facilitator will take the lead in delivering content and engaging participants, while the other facilitator will act in the role of "producer" to manage technology, run breakout groups, and support the content as dictated by the facilitator guide.

Using a synchronous format, via the virtual classroom, ensures that the facilitator stays involved with the participants during the learning process. This is a key concern of ABC Company. The class design and facilitator guide will integrate the responsibility of both facilitators to create a seamless delivery.

A participant workbook also needs to be developed to support the synchronous activities and provide instructions for the on-the-job practice activities. This workbook needs to be tightly integrated into the synchronous design, and will serve as a useful tool after the new hire training is complete.

The two facilitators who once taught together in the physical classroom will now be responsible for teaching together in the synchronous classroom, but the experience will be much different. In the physical classroom format, the person who was not in charge of the content at a particular moment did not need to be present. In the synchronous environment, the facilitators will be online together throughout all of the online sessions. They will need to rehearse and prepare prior to each session, and learn to work within a "team-teaching" framework rather than as two independent facilitators supporting the same curriculum.

Schedule

The new hires will participate in a synchronous session four times a week for two weeks. The sessions will be approximately two hours in length. This maximum program time (assuming strong facilitation and design) will allow participants to stay focused without becoming restless. Similar to the recommended asynchronous format proposed in chapter 5, the schedule will allow the new hire sales training content to be augmented with on-the-job activities that help to reinforce the concepts (see Table 6-10 at the end of this chapter). And, similar to the recommended asynchronous format, the unallocated time will be spent completing structured activities such as learning how to use the Customer Relationship Management system (using tutorials from the vendor), reviewing and contributing to the sales training wikis and blogs, and meeting with the office administrator to learn how to utilize office resources such as email, proposal templates, and sales tracking software.

The synchronous approach starts to combine the best of the classroom format and the asynchronous format. New hires will have the advantage of learning from a live facilitator, while at the same time learning in smaller chunks, and having the ability to interact with their office colleagues on a day-to-day basis.

NEWLY DESIGNED SYNCHRONOUS OBJECTIVES AND DESIGN CONSIDERATIONS

As in the previous chapter, the synchronous design will look at each individual objective and propose a learning approach that best achieves that objective.

Objective 1

Table 6-1 illustrates Objective 1: Represent the organization in a professional manner.

Table 6-1. Represent the Organization in a Professional Manner

Old Objective	New Objective	Rationale
See new objective.	1. Represent the organization in a professional manner. 1.1 Define professionalism. 1.2 Select attire that conforms to company guidelines. 1.3 Develop rapport in a way that creates a comfortable environment.	This objective was culled from the old objective that stated: Demonstrate the ability to open a sales call and *behave in a professional manner.* This objective was created as a stand-alone objective because behaving in a professional manner should be a core skill regardless of what task an individual is performing. The organization considers this an important objective to call out and practice because the majority of new hires come directly from college and have limited professional experience.

Synchronous Design Approach. Using a synchronous approach allows participants to be collaborative throughout the learning process, and the initial online session for new salespeople will provide the opportunity for the participants to become comfortable working with their peers, and the facilitators, over a distance.

The initial session will be low pressure, focused on learning how to be an effective online participant while getting to know the other members of the cohort. Expectations for the curriculum will be set, and the technology tool set will be introduced. Figure 6-2 is an example of a whiteboard on which participants will introduce themselves using the whiteboard tools in a grid format. This collaborative exercise has several functions: It allows all participants to provide their opinion (not just the first person who raises a hand); it keeps the program active by providing an opportunity to interact with the tool and with other learners; and it provides the facilitator information to which to react.

In their pre-assigned box, trainees will type several words that come to mind when they think of the word *professionalism*. The facilitator will debrief this exercise by calling on at least four people to explain their concepts in more

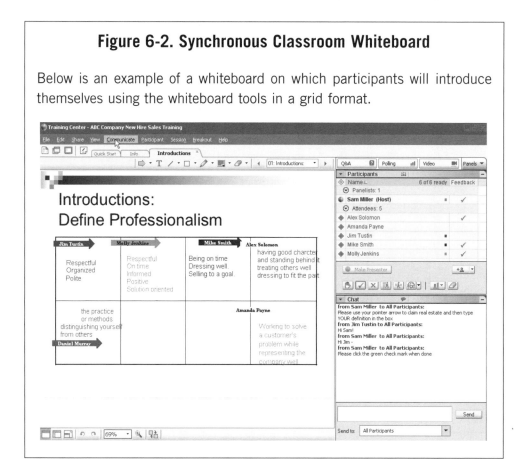

Figure 6-2. Synchronous Classroom Whiteboard

Below is an example of a whiteboard on which participants will introduce themselves using the whiteboard tools in a grid format.

detail. Before these four "volunteers" explain their comments, they will introduce themselves to the rest of the group. (Throughout the rest of the session, the other participants will have the opportunity to introduce themselves when they contribute verbally to the conversation for the first time.) This conversation will conclude by the facilitator providing ABC Company's definition of *professionalism.*

After this formal exercise, participants will have an opportunity to introduce themselves by sharing one trait about themselves that their colleagues can count on for assistance or support, such as, "I am very good at time management." A copy of this completed whiteboard will be saved and distributed, so all participants can start to develop relationships and rapport with the other members of their group. (Knowing that there are 12 people on whom you can rely can certainly be comforting when starting a new job.)

The session will conclude with a video of the president of ABC Company talking about its history and reputation and the importance for all new hires to uphold that reputation through their dress, their speech, their interactions with clients, and in the community at large.

As with the asynchronous approach, the synchronous design does not fully address the interpersonal nature of this objective. Items like "building rapport in a face-to-face setting" and "Utilizing body language and eye contact" are skills that require practice in order to master. The synchronous environment cannot effectively duplicate the face-to-face setting; therefore, any realistic assessment must be done outside the primary classroom environment. These interpersonal skills will be assessed at the very end of the curriculum. The culminating activity for participants, after all training has been completed, will be to schedule and make a presentation to fellow, more experienced, salespeople in their field offices. The presentation also will assess all of the presentation-oriented objectives, and will allow colleagues to quiz participants on product knowledge and sales situations.

To practice for this portion of the presentation, participants will be provided with a "Body Language and Eye Contact Tip Sheet" (see chapter 5), which will provide advice on things like shaking hands, maintaining good posture, maintaining appropriate distance, and eye contact. This tip sheet will be accompanied by a short evaluation form that participants can use to assess people they speak to over the next several weeks. This same evaluation form will be used during their final presentation as part of their own personal assessment.

Impact on Participants. In this initial session, participants will start to become comfortable in the synchronous classroom. They will have the opportunity to meet the other members of their cohort, and discuss the professional standards of ABC Company.

The initial discussion will focus on the concept of professionalism, which is a positive way to start any new job. Also, with a synchronous approach, training will be kicked off in a very active way. Participants will be contributing before the instructor even begins to speak. They will do this by interacting with the virtual classroom tools, writing on the whiteboard, and texting one another to start building rapport.

Impact on Design. A learning orientation for the virtual classroom needs to be developed to expedite the participant's transition into learning in the synchronous space. This orientation is something that can be used across the organization, not just for the new hire sales training program.

A short web-ready video (less than five minutes) will be produced, which features the president of ABC Company welcoming the new salespeople and emphasizing the need to represent the organization in a professional manner.

A "Body Language and Eye Contact Tip Sheet" and evaluation form will need to be created for participants to use to evaluate the body language and eye contact of colleagues and acquaintances they speak with during the course of the training.

Impact on Facilitation Team. The facilitation team will need to work hard to get to know participants during this first session. They must build rapport and create an atmosphere in which the participants can successfully learn. If the facilitators stumble with the technology or do not work together effectively, it will set a negative tone for the entire curriculum.

Salespeople need to have personalities that allow them to jump right into conversations, no matter how awkward or new a situation is, and during this kickoff session, the facilitators will be able to encourage those important interaction skills immediately.

Impact on the Organization. When participants begin their tenure at an organization by learning in a virtual classroom, it will set their expectations for the learning culture at the organization. Once a critical mass of new hires has been trained in this fashion, it will become the learning "norm" for all programs.

Impact on the Job. As in the asynchronous approach, allowing the participants to learn from their desks means that they are interacting in their offices immediately. The in-depth discussion around professionalism will help participants begin their new careers with an understanding of the expected standards with regard to dress, behavior, and communication.

Assessment Plan. "Representing the organization in a professional manner" is an interpersonal skill. The new hire salespeople will ultimately be expected to interact outside of a classroom format with prospects and clients; because of this, the facilitators cannot effectively gauge the mastery of this objective in the synchronous format. It will be left up to the sales managers and office colleagues to ensure that professionalism is being exhibited in a final presentation after the training is complete. The participants' presentation to their colleagues will demonstrate, in accordance with the fulfillment of Objective 1, their understanding of professional dress, their skill at rapport building, and their ability to utilize effective eye contact and body language.

Objective 2

Table 6-2 illustrates Objective 2: Describe the features and benefits of the company's five core products to prospective buyers.

Table 6-2. Describe the Features and Benefits of the Company's Five Core Products to Prospective Buyers

Old Objective	New Objective	Rationale
Describe our basic product offering.	2. Describe the features and benefits of the company's five core products to prospective buyers. 2.1 What are the core products of each? 2.2 What are the features and benefits? 2.3 Identify which product most closely aligns with a prospect's needs.	The original objective was vague, and not complete. What do we mean by "describe"? To whom? What should be included? Does each prospect receive the same description? Also, the phrase "basic product offering" was left to interpretation. The company carries more than 30 products—which are to be considered "basic"? The new objective addresses these questions.

Synchronous Design Approach. Prior to attending the synchronous session focused on this objective, participants will use their workbooks to review ABC Company's core products. The live session will kick off with a quiz designed to ensure the participants understand which products make up the core offerings. (While pre-reading is technically an asynchronous technique, using a workbook to inform a participant about knowledge-based objectives is the best practice in synchronous training. Long lectures designed to simply convey information are considered an ineffective use of the technology.)

After the quiz is debriefed, the facilitators will conduct a short discussion regarding the distinction between features and benefits. The participants will be divided into five groups and sent to virtual breakout rooms. Each group will be required to come up with a list of features and benefits for one of the core products. The features and benefits lists will be debriefed in a large group, with the facilitator providing missing information and identifying items that should not be on the lists.

During the next synchronous session, the participants will work in the same breakout teams to address case studies. Each case will introduce a prospect profile. Members of the breakout group will work together to determine which product or products most closely align with a prospect's needs, and prepare a short presentation to support the decision. The presentation will be made to the larger group when the breakout room work is finished.

Impact on Participants. While mastering this objective, participants will have the opportunity to combine independent research with group work. Participants will need to rely on one another to be successful, which will continue to lay the foundation for a strong network across this distributed cohort. A case study analysis allows the participants to apply critical thinking and problem solving in regard to a potential prospect.

Impact on Design. The workbook will strongly support this learning objective. It will contain product descriptions for the five core products that the participants are to review independently. It also will contain technical instructions and activity instructions for the breakout room, so the participants will be successful while working on their own (every time a breakout room is used in this design, the workbook will support the activity in this manner). The workbook also will provide guidelines for groups to make their presentations to the full class.

Impact on Facilitation Team. Because of the collaborative nature of the activities used to support this objective, facilitators will have very active roles. They will need to be involved with the debrief presentations, filling knowledge gaps, and supporting individual breakout teams.

Impact on the Organization. As participants learn to collaborate using the virtual classroom technology, they are preparing to collaborate company-wide. A case study analysis activity will illustrate the benefits of working with a colleague to brainstorm solutions.

Impact on the Job. Because product research and determination of features and benefits were completed by the participants, not delivered via lecture by facilitators, participants will begin their jobs with a more ingrained understanding of the core products of ABC Company.

Assessment Plan. The initial assessment is designed to ensure that participants understand the core products of the company based on an independent reading assignment. The expectation is that participants will score almost perfectly on the short assessment. Those trainees who do not will be contacted by a facilitator later in the day, at which time the facilitator will encourage them to be more prepared in future sessions. By contacting these participants individually, we feel that they will understand that their individual performance makes a difference not only on the job, but also in training.

Objective 3

Table 6-3 illustrates Objective 3: Compare and contrast the company's core products with the products of our three closest competitors.

Table 6-3. Compare and Contrast the Company's Core Products With the Products of Our Three Closest Competitors

Old Objective	New Objective	Rationale
Compare and contrast our product and sales platform with our three closest competitors.	3. Compare and contrast the company's core products to the products of our three closest competitors. 3.1 Identify closest competitors, including characteristics that define them as closest competitors. 3.2 Identify competitor offerings that most closely align with our own. 3.3 Compare similarities and contrast differences between the competitor's products and our core products.	The original objective contained jargon ("sales platform") that not even the sales managers could define; so that language was removed. In addition, it is ambitious to assume that new hires can leave the program being able to discuss more than 30 products; so the objective now references the core products, identified in Objective 2.

Synchronous Design Approach. For salespeople to be successful, they must be knowledgeable not only about the products and services they are selling, but also about competitors' products. This session will warm up with a brainstorming activity, identifying those companies the participants think are the closest competitors of ABC Company. The facilitator will then provide the correct list of competitors, highlighting sales numbers, target client audience, and other key demographic information. Guided by their workbooks, participants will independently search the Internet for these competitors and identify the offerings that most closely align with the key offerings of ABC Company. This activity will be the "Key Competitor Product Scavenger Hunt."

Participants will then work in pairs in breakout rooms. Each team will be assigned a competitor and an ABC core product with which to work. After 20 minutes, participants will be reconvened in a larger group, and each team will present their analysis. The facilitators will provide feedback as appropriate.

Impact on Participants. The treatment of this objective continues to reinforce that salespeople will be responsible for doing a large part of their own research. While the company might provide some core information about key competitors, it is up to the individual salesperson to ensure that he or she has the right information and also to be able to compare and contrast offerings from new competitors or new products from existing competitors.

Impact on Design. A "Key Competitor Product Scavenger Hunt" needs to be created for the workbook. Also, an Internet research checklist will be created to support participants in this activity. This information needs to be reviewed prior to each delivery of the new hire sales training, as data about competitors and their products may have changed.

Impact on Facilitation Team. This is another highly facilitated objective. The facilitators will need to act as guides and coaches throughout the research and presentation phase.

Impact on the Organization. In addition to learning about competitors and their products, participants will continue to practice their research, collaboration, and presentation skills. While research and collaboration are not official objectives of the curriculum, they are skills that will help the salespeople to be successful. By incorporating these types of activities throughout the curriculum, the organization will minimize the need to provide additional training in supplemental areas.

Impact on the Job. The synchronous design allows participants to learn on their own, in a facilitated format. Instead of being told about the competitors, participants will leave the training class with the skills they need to conduct further research on their own.

Assessment Plan. The facilitator will be able to assess the participants' mastery of this objective by observing the presentations made by the teams. If the team did not thoroughly research or present their findings in an effective manner, they will be given that feedback by the facilitator in the presentation debrief.

Objective 4

Table 6-4 illustrates Objective 4: Target high-potential prospects.

Table 6-4. Target High-Potential Prospects

Old Objective	New Objective	Rationale
Describe the characteristics of a viable prospect.	4. Target high-potential prospects. 4.1 Describe the characteristics of a viable prospect. 4.2 Develop a prioritized prospecting list. 4.3 Create a customized approach to engage the prospect in a sales conversation.	The original objective did not take this concept far enough. A salesperson must do more than describe a viable prospect; he or she must identify prospects and then find a way to engage them.

Synchronous Design Approach. Prior to attending the session, participants will complete a questionnaire based on interviews with colleagues in their office. The interview will consist of questions about existing clients, and will help the new hire identify what constitutes a viable prospect. The questionnaire also will help participants uncover how the more experienced salespeople in their offices determine how to pursue a prospect, including the selection criteria used to make those determinations.

This session will open with a whiteboard exercise that will allow participants to share the best piece of advice received from a person in their field office, as well as stories about the advice, if time permits.

The "meat" of this topic will be based on the Profiling and Qualifying Tool, which was created by one of the facilitators to support the existing classroom design (see chapter 4). The tool helps participants profile ideal prospects and enables them to understand that not all prospects are viable custom-ers. The tool will discuss such things as minimum employee size, minimum number of locations considered to be ideal in a prospect, and parameters for company earnings.

After learning how to use the tool, and watching the facilitator walk through an example, participants will be referred to their workbooks, which contain profiles of 10 potential prospects. Using the tool, they will prioritize the prospects to categorize those that are most likely to need ABC Company's products *and* buy from the organization. Participants then complete the rank-ordering activity using the 10 profiles, and finally, all participants meet in a synchronous classroom, which begins with a poll asking the participants to share their final prioritized list of prospects to pursue. A large group debrief will follow this independent "ideal prospect" activity, so that participants can compare their lists and share their rationale for ordering their lists.

Impact on Participants. The goal of this objective is to help new hire salespeople to be self-sufficient once they return to their field offices and are assigned a territory. The prospecting tool and the thought process involved in the prioritization of the profile examples will help participants understand the questions they should ask, and the decisions they should make, to maximize their selling time and have the most success in closing sales.

To successfully master this objective, participants need to show initiative in collecting viable prospect data prior to the class. In addition, they will need to stay focused during a relatively long (30-minute) self-paced exercise. They will find that, even as new hires, there are many distractions to pull them away from completing desk work.

Impact on Design. The tool has already been created thanks to one of the facilitators, but it may need to be tweaked a bit once the ideal prospect charac-teristics are vetted with a number of field office managers. The profiles handout will need to be created from scratch; this should not be difficult, as every sales manager would certainly have a client that could be profiled in this manner.

Impact on Facilitation Team. The delivery of this topic is something that the facilitator, Sam, is already used to as he utilizes the tool in the current classroom design when speaking about the topic of prospecting. Facilitators will need to understand the "correct" order of the prospect list and the ratio-nale behind that order to help participants better understand the decisions that should be made when choosing whether or not to pursue a prospect. The facilitators will stay "on the line" and in the classroom to assist participants who may have questions.

Impact on the Organization. Formalizing the use of the Profiling and Quali-fying Tool will help ensure that salespeople are using the same basic criteria for selecting prospects company-wide. Other factors will affect whether or not to pursue a prospect—we cannot rely on the objectiveness of the tool alone. However, utilizing a common tool is a good first step toward identifying a viable prospect.

Impact on the Job. This profiling process should enable new salespeople to succeed more quickly because they are pursuing only qualified leads.

Assessment Plan. This topic will not be formally assessed, as it would be difficult to determine if someone truly has the critical skills necessary to identify good prospects until he or she has been on the job for at least two months and has had the opportunity to research and profile a number of prospects in a given territory.

Objective 5

Table 6-5 illustrates Objective 5: Demonstrate the ability to open a sales call.

Table 6-5. Demonstrate the Ability to Open a Sales Call

Old Objective	New Objective	Rationale
Demonstrate the ability to open a sales call and behave in a professional manner.	5. Demonstrate the ability to open a sales call. 5.1 Greet the prospect. 5.2 Propose an agenda for the meeting, state the value to the prospect, and check that the prospect accepts your agenda. 5.3 Ask questions that uncover the prospect's true need.	"Behave in a professional manner" was determined to be an independent objective and is now addressed in Objective 1. The steps involved in opening a sales call are now defined so that they can be more clearly assessed.

Synchronous Design Approach. This topic will be taught via the use of a video and a role play. Utilizing the virtual classroom browser and computer speakers, participants will watch five vignettes of salespeople opening various sales calls with potential clients. Each vignette will be followed by a short discussion about what the salesperson demonstrated, how it was received by the prospect, and why that might be a good initial opening to a sales call. Once the participants feel confident about the process of opening a sales call, they will break into groups of three to role-play this skill, using a breakout room. Each individual will practice opening a sales call twice. When not practicing in the role of salesperson, the other trainees in each team will either play the role of the prospect or will make notes as an observer of the practice interaction.

Following the role play, a large group discussion will be conducted asking the participants to brainstorm questions to uncover a prospect's needs. The participants will use their workbooks to make note of the appropriate type of questions used to uncover prospect needs. A short lecture on the difference between open-ended and closed-ended questions will be incorporated.

Impact on Participants. Not only will the participants be able to see appropriate sales call opening techniques modeled by various individuals in different situations, they will be able to practice emulating the same techniques themselves. This approach gives them a number of best practice examples as well as the opportunity to internalize the process and the dialogue via practice.

One downside is that participants will not be able to react to or use body language and eye contact to make their point. The facilitator will encourage participants to practice these role plays in front of a mirror, a family member, or a colleague—any avenue that will allow the salesperson to gauge and respond to physical reactions.

The final activity, brainstorming appropriate questions, will assist new salespeople in getting to the next level. It is not enough to have a good opening dialogue; it is essential that the salesperson also know what kinds of questions to ask and what kind of information to gather from a prospect to make an informed decision about whether or not to continue to pursue the prospect.

Impact on Design. A commercial video, in digital format (so that it can be broadcast via the web), that demonstrates opening and closing a sales call will be purchased. In addition, role-play roles and an observation checklist will be created.

Impact on Facilitation Team. This training approach is particularly beneficial for the facilitators because, while this topic certainly could be taught in lecture format, or the two facilitators themselves could demonstrate appropriate sales call openings, seeing a number of examples and a number of different approaches as portrayed in the video has more impact. The facilitators will need to be skilled at the debriefing of each vignette to clearly call to the participants' attention the process and technique each vignette demonstrates, and they will need to be available to navigate through the breakout rooms to assist the teams during the practice role plays to ensure that they stay on task and are practicing the appropriate dialogue correctly.

Impact on the Organization. The organization will benefit from salespeople who have had an opportunity to practice this skill before opening a sales call with an actual prospect.

Impact on the Job. Opening a sales call and being able to interact with various personality styles of business people is a technique that can be perfected only with practice and time. The participants' ability to practice during the role play will be beneficial but will not be extensive enough to allow them to truly master opening a sales call. The list of questions generated during the brainstorming exercise will be a handy reference for new hires once they are back on the job.

Assessment Plan. The role play acts as an assessment, as it gives each individual the ability to demonstrate his or her understanding of the required skills and receive feedback from a fellow participant. The feedback form that is used during the training may also be forwarded to an individual sales manager, so that the sales manager can continue to assess and hone the skills of each new hire assigned to his or her office.

Objective 6

Table 6-6 illustrates Objective 6: Demonstrate the ability to manage a prospect meeting.

Table 6-6. Demonstrate the Ability to Manage a Prospect Meeting

Old Objective	New Objective	Rationale
See new objective.	6. Demonstrate the ability to manage a prospect meeting. 6.1 Probe for clarification. 6.2 Suggest solutions that meet the need.	This objective was added because, effectively, the course had been teaching salespeople enough to get in the door, but not providing them the skills they needed after they arrived. The new objective attempts to assist salespeople in managing the meeting and working with the prospect to devise a solution that ultimately results in a sale.

Synchronous Design Approach. This topic is, in essence, a continuation of the prior topic, now asking participants to put together their ability to ask appropriate questions to gain more information about the prospect and his or her organization, and then suggest an ABC product or service that meets the needs of the prospect.

The participants will work in triads in the breakout rooms. Each triad will be provided with a completed Profiling and Qualifying Tool for a representative company and will create a strategy to manage the meeting. The groups will spend 10 minutes determining

- the goals for the meeting (get the sale, get a meeting with a different department, set up a second meeting)
- questions that need to be answered by the prospect
- a strategy for keeping the prospect's interest throughout the call.

Each group will then present their approach to the class, and receive feedback and advice to strengthen their strategies.

Impact on Participants. This is a very experiential approach that will allow participants to think strategically and apply what they have learned early in the class. The approach also will allow participants to continue practicing their presentation skills.

Impact on Design. At least six case studies need to be developed, resulting in completed Profiling and Qualifying Tools for each potential triad group. The workbook needs to contain very specific instructions for working in the breakout groups, so triads can work independently.

Impact on Facilitation Team. The facilitators will support the individual breakout room teams to help prepare the presentation, and then provide feedback during the group presentations, taking the point of view of the prospect.

Impact on the Organization. The organization will have a more confident salesforce that understands more completely the nature of the sales process.

Impact on the Job. This process should lead to more closed sales because the salesperson will understand how to maintain an effective dialogue with a prospect. However, time on the job and more realistic practice opportunities will be needed for the participant to truly be successful.

Assessment Plan. The case study presentation will inform the facilitators as to the level of audience understanding.

Objective 7

Table 6-7 illustrates Objective 7: Demonstrate the ability to close a sales call.

Table 6-7. Demonstrate the Ability to Close a Sales Call

Old Objective	New Objective	Rationale
See new objective.	7. Demonstrate the ability to close a sales call. 7.1 Confirm that the meeting has met the prospect's expectation. 7.2 Close the call with suggested next steps and timelines.	This new objective is included to ensure that a salesperson can effectively close a sales call. This was not addressed in the original training.

Synchronous Design Approach. Most often a sale is lost simply because a salesperson never asks for the sale. This topic culminates the sales call process by teaching participants how to successfully close a sale. An online video of sales closing vignettes will be used and each vignette debriefed, as in Objective 5, which will help the participants understand the dialogue they might hear indicating that a prospect is willing to close the sales process. A final round of role plays will be conducted in breakout rooms, which will assist the participants in bringing together the entire process: opening a sales call, gathering information by asking appropriate questions, offering solutions by targeting specific products or services to the prospect's expressed needs, and finally asking for the sale and suggesting next steps.

Impact on Participants. Participants will see and hear best practices and dissect them for the techniques that they should emulate. They will then be able to practice the entire sales call process from beginning to end, which will help them to understand and internalize their role in the sales call process.

Impact on Design. This is effectively the same exercise that was used for the previous objective, and a similar video or format will be used. Again, role-play roles and an online observation checklist will need to be created.

Impact on Facilitation Team. The facilitators will need to be skilled at the debriefing of each vignette to clearly call to the participants' attention the process and technique each vignette demonstrates, and they will need to be available to navigate through the breakout rooms to assist the teams during the practice role plays to ensure that they stay on task and are practicing the appropriate dialogue correctly.

Impact on the Organization. The organization will benefit from salespeople who have had an opportunity to practice this skill before closing a sales call with an actual prospect.

Impact on the Job. The participants' ability to practice during the role play will be beneficial but will not be extensive enough to allow them to truly master closing a sales call. More practice will be required, on the job.

Assessment Plan. The role play acts as an assessment, as it gives each individual the ability to demonstrate his or her understanding of the required skills and receive feedback from a fellow participant. The feedback form that is used during the training may also be forwarded to an individual sales manager, so that the sales manager can continue to assess and hone the skills of each new hire.

Objective 8

Table 6-8 illustrates Objective 8: Manage objections.

Table 6-8. Manage Objections

Old Objective	New Objective	Rationale
Respond to objections in an appropriate manner.	8. Manage objections. 8.1 Identify an objection. 8.2 Categorize the objection. 8.3 Respond to the objection in a way that keeps the conversation moving forward.	This objective was reworded to align with Objectives 6 and 7.

Synchronous Design Approach. An ongoing assignment for the participants, throughout the program, will be to gather objections that prospects have stated when asked to invest in ABC Company's products. After each live session, the facilitator will remind participants to pay attention to experienced colleagues' schedules and find opportunities to talk to them after prospect calls. Participants will keep a log of common (and uncommon) objections. Participants should ask how their colleagues overcame those objections, if indeed they did.

Prior to the synchronous session focused on managing objections, participants will create a PowerPoint slide listing five to 10 different objections, and submit their slides to the facilitator. The facilitator will categorize the objections and create four different slides containing representative objections from each category. Categories might include time, expense, and an existing contract with another company.

The live session will open with a conversation about how to effectively respond to an objection, using guidance and examples provided by the participant workbook. Then, the facilitator will begin to put participants on the spot by bringing up an objection and requiring participants to call on their knowledge of ABC Company's products and services, their features and benefits, and how they would best align with a prospect's expressed needs to respond to the objection. After the participant has responded, it will be up to another participant to debrief and provide feedback on the effectiveness of the response. This ensures that everyone stays focused on the activity to respond appropriately. Final feedback will be provided by the facilitator. This will be repeated until everyone has had the opportunity to respond.

Impact on Participants. Participants will have the opportunity to craft responses to realistic prospect objections. They also will have the opportunity to interact with their office colleagues to collect the objections and, in the process, start to strengthen relationships with the people in their offices.

Impact on Design. This design requires a participant to start thinking about objections long before the topic comes up in a live session. The live session will consist of a short lecture and then an open-ended discussion. The success of the synchronous learning approach depends on the ability of the facilitator to keep the conversation moving. A job aid with typical objections and responses should be designed for distribution after the session.

Impact on Facilitation Team. The design of this content will require both facilitators to manage time effectively, while ensuring that all typical objections are aired and everyone has an opportunity to respond. The facilitators will distribute a "Typical Objections Job Aid" after the session.

Impact on the Organization. Having salespeople who are confident in knowing that an objection does not mean "no" will lead to increased sales, because these salespeople will continue longer in the sales process than those who hear their first objection and, at that point, end the sales process with the prospect.

Impact on the Job. As a result of this training process, ABC Company's new hire salespeople will have better success at closing sales because they will understand that an objection is a natural part of the selling process, and they will be appropriately prepared to respond to objections of various types. They also will be more likely to rely on fellow salespeople in their field office, as well as their colleagues across the country, when they are faced with a particularly difficult objection because the training process fostered that cooperative relationship.

Assessment Plan. Assessing the participants' success at recognizing and categorizing objections will be done during the learning process (the online activity). However, being able to respond appropriately to an objection in a static environment is entirely different from being faced with an actual objection during the sales process. The true measure of success will be the number of sales each salesperson is able to close, as well as how quickly the sales process is closed, once the new hire is on the job.

Objective 9

Table 6-9 illustrates Objective 9: Implement an action plan designed to meet quota in the specified time period.

Table 6-9. Implement an Action Plan Designed to Meet Quota in the Specified Time Period

Old Objective	New Objective	Rationale
Set sales goals for self that align with quotas and sales manager expectations.	9. Implement an action plan designed to meet quota in the specified time period. 9.1 Articulate quota requirements. 9.2 Calculate what is necessary for you to meet your quota. 9.3 Create a list of "to-dos," with timelines. 9.4 Plan an agenda for a meeting with your supervisor to review and amend your plan. 9.5 Monitor and update action plan as necessary, to ensure you stay on track.	The original objective implied that salespeople would be responsible for setting their own sales goals. This is not the case. Salespeople need to understand the sales quota requirements, and create a plan to meet (or exceed) those requirements. The new objective addresses this need, and incorporates working with managers to assist and guide.

Synchronous Design Approach. This topic will begin with a field office sales manager discussing the sales goal process. Topics include how quotas are assigned, the typical success trajectory of a new salesperson, time management best practices, and the compensation system. The participants will be encouraged to ask questions regarding their role and the expectations of the sales managers. This will be an informal discussion to allow participants to be comfortable with an individual in a management role and begin to see him or her as a coach and a support system rather than as a task assigner or school principal.

The sales manager will then discuss how he or she would approach working with a new hire to implement goals and help the new hire be successful.

Given a template that will include a timeline or organizer, each trainee will have a one-on-one meeting with his or her sales manager to set appropriate interim goals during their first three months on the job. While the six-month sales quota is not negotiable, interim goals for reaching quota can differ from sales manager to sales manager.

Participants will reconvene for the last synchronous session to compare and contrast the expectations of the various managers.

Impact on Participants. Participants will have a better expectation of how their particular sales manager will assess, monitor, and support their performance.

Impact on Design. A fill-in-the-blank goal-setting template will be created for this portion of the learning process.

Impact on Facilitation Team. The facilitator will take on the role of a coach, encouraging new hires to develop the plan for success.

Impact on the Organization. New hire salespeople should be more successful, earlier in their careers, as a result of the training process occurring in the sales office, which affords the participants the ability to experience sales calls, understand how a sales office operates, and develop a relationship with their manager much sooner than if they had attended a training class at the corporate headquarters.

Impact on the Job. Participants should have more success reaching their six-month sales quota. New hires also should see their sales manager as a resource in assisting them to achieve their quota and become a successful salesperson within that manager's field office.

Assessment Plan. Ultimately, the assessment of goal setting and action planning will be whether or not more new hires achieve their sales goal than they have in the past.

CONCLUSION

The proposed synchronous design is eminently viable at ABC Company—the costs of production are low, the synchronous sessions are spread out over a period of a little more than two weeks, and the materials developed for the program are reusable. The role plays start to get new hires familiar with making sales calls; however, they are not realistic in that the situations are contrived and the practice does not happen face-to-face.

Because there are several exercises that require new hires to interact with their office colleagues, this design starts to create relationships with the people new hires work with every day.

DELIVERABLE TO CLIENT

The training agenda found in Table 6-10 outlines the synchronous training process and the tools needed to achieve success via the synchronous training delivery method. In our discussion with the client, we will emphasize the benefits of a synchronous delivery in terms of the immediate transfer of new knowledge and skills to the workplace and the benefits of breaking the learning content into two-hour chunks, which allows for learning, practice, application and reflection, and learning again.

IN THE NEXT CHAPTER

This chapter provided a detailed discussion of creating synchronous learning that met the nine established learning objectives established for new hire sales training at ABC Company. You have no doubt noticed that many activities that are done in a physical classroom can be replicated in a virtual classroom. This is because we are concentrating on the learning outcomes of a learning objective and not on the delivery medium. Good instructional design is good instructional design—the modality is adaptable.

The next chapter discusses the pros and cons of choosing a blended approach that incorporates selected elements of the methodologies discussed in chapters 4, 5, and 6. Pay particular attention to the choices recommended to ABC Company for a blended offering. The emphasis is always on matching a particular objective with the delivery methodology that would best serve the learner and the organization: knowledge items are delivered asynchronously, skill items are delivered synchronously, and the application of new knowledge and skill is done in an on-the-job setting.

Table 6-10. New Hire Sales Training Program

Daily Activities	Time Required	Resources Required
Ongoing		
Evaluate body language of office colleagues.	Up to five hours over a two-week period	Body Language and Eye Contact Tip Sheet Form to evaluate colleagues' eye contact and body language
Interview office colleagues about what makes a good prospect.	Up to three hours over a one-week period	Colleague Questionnaire: What makes a good prospect?
Interview office colleagues about common objections.	Up to three hours over a two-week period	Colleague Questionnaire: What are common objections to buying our products?
Week 1		
Day 1 1. Trainees will participate in an introductory session that teaches technology, sets expectations for the new hire curriculum, and introduces participants. 2. Participants will watch a welcome video from president of ABC Company and discuss with cohort.	Two hours	Virtual Classroom Video Synchronous learning orientation New hire training workbook

(continued on page 142)

Table 6-10. New Hire Sales Training Program (continued)

Daily Activities	Time Required	Resources Required
Day 2 1. Participants will spend the morning reviewing ABC Company's core products in workbook. 2. Trainees will participate in a synchronous session that addresses ABC Company core products. 3. Participants will engage in a breakout room activity to brainstorm features and benefits of core products.	Two hours reviewing products Ninety minutes in synchronous session	Virtual Classroom Quiz on core products New hire training workbook
Day 3 1. Participants will work in a synchronous breakout room to develop prospect case studies. Teams will determine which products best meet the prospect's needs and make a presentation to the larger group that supports their decision.	Two hours	Virtual Classroom New hire training workbook
Day 4 1. Participants will work in the synchronous classroom to identify key competitors. 2. After short group exercises, participants will spend 15 minutes completing the "Key Competitor Product Scavenger Hunt," which will help participants identify the competitor offerings that most closely align with ABC Company's products.	Three hours	Virtual Classroom New hire training workbook Key Competitor Product Scavenger Hunt, with Internet research checklist to support activity

Daily Activities	Time Required	Resources Required
3. Participants will work in pairs to analyze a competitor and create a presentation on that competitor to the larger group.		
Day 5 1. In the synchronous classroom, participants will share the best piece of advice they received from their office colleagues concerning what makes a good prospect. 2. The facilitator will demonstrate how to use the Profiling and Qualifying Tool. 3. The participants will use the tool to independently prioritize 10 prospects in their workbooks, followed by a group debrief to compare notes. 4. Each participant should make an appointment with their sales manager for the afternoon of Day 10 to complete an action plan.	Two hours	Virtual Classroom Colleague Questionnaire: What makes a good prospect? Profiling and Qualifying Tool New hire training workbook

(continued on page 144)

Table 6-10. New Hire Sales Training Program (continued)

Daily Activities	Time Required	Resources Required
Week 2 *Day 6* 1. In the morning virtual classroom session, participants will watch a video on how to open a sales call. 2. Participants will address discussion questions for each video vignette with facilitator and the group. 3. In breakout teams of three, each participant will practice opening a sales call at least two times. 4. In the afternoon virtual classroom session, participants will brainstorm questions to uncover a prospect's needs. A lecture on question types will be included.	Two live sessions Session 1—two hours Session 2—one hour	Virtual Classroom Opening a sales call video, accessible via a website New hire training workbook Practice exercises
Day 7 1. Participants will work in groups of three in breakout rooms to create a strategy to manage a fictional prospect meeting, and then present their approach to the larger groups.	Three hours	Virtual Classroom Fictional prospects presented in a Profiling and Qualifying Tool

Daily Activities	Time Required	Resources Required
Day 8 1. In a virtual classroom session, participants will watch a video on how to close a sales call. 2. Participants will address discussion questions for each video vignette with facilitator and the group. 3. In breakout teams of three, each participant will practice the entire sales process, including opening a call, asking questions, offering solutions, and asking for the sale during closing. 4. On their own time, participants will create a PowerPoint presentation containing five to 10 common objections identified by office colleagues. This presentation should be submitted to the facilitator by 3:00 p.m. Eastern time.	Three hours	Virtual Classroom Closing a sales call video, accessible via a website New hire training workbook Practice exercises Job aid summarizing the steps of the sales process
Day 9 1. In the virtual classroom, the facilitator will present a compilation of the common objections submitted by participants on the previous day. Each participant will have the opportunity to respond to an objection, and get feedback as to the effectiveness of the response. 2. Participants will receive a job aid of typical objections and their responses after the session is finished.	Two hours	Virtual Classroom Job aid with typical objections and responses

(continued on page 146)

Table 6-10. New Hire Sales Training Program (continued)

Daily Activities	Time Required	Resources Required
Day 10 1. In the virtual classroom, a sales manager will give a short presentation on the sales goal process. 2. After the session, each participant will complete a sales goals action plan with his or her sales manager. 3. Each participant will schedule a final presentation with his or her office colleagues, to take place in approximately one week.	Four hours	Virtual Classroom software Sales manager guest speaker Sales Goals Action planning template Instructions for setting up final presentation
Day 11 1. Participants will meet for a final synchronous session to compare and contrast the expectations of their sales managers, and to wrap up the New Hire Sales Training Program. 2. The final presentation expectations will be discussed.	Two hours	Virtual Classroom Instructions for setting up final presentation
Days 12–15 Prepare for next week's presentation.	Full day, as needed	Access to all learning resources, senior salesperson, sales manager

Week 3

Presentation

You will prepare a presentation to your sales office that summarizes the top three things you have learned (from learning experiences, sales calls, conversations with more senior salespeople, your training facilitator, your manager, and your peers), and demonstrates your presentation skills encompassing eye contact, appropriate body language, and questioning skills. Your fellow salespeople will evaluate you on your knowledge of ABC Company products, your presentation abilities, and your ability to respond to questions or objections.

An evaluation form will be completed, and collected by your sales manager, to provide you feedback in the following areas: presentation skills, product knowledge, and handling objections. Your sales manager may require you to give this presentation again if you do not meet minimum requirements. Once the presentation is complete, you are considered a full-fledged member of your sales office and your six-month timeframe to meet your quota goal begins.

Congratulations and good luck!

Chapter 7

Blending in Three Dimensions: Meeting Participant, Instructional, and Organizational Needs

This chapter discusses the pros and cons of choosing a blended approach that intertwines elements of the three methodologies discussed in the previous chapters: classroom-based, asynchronous, and synchronous training. As with the previous chapters, this discussion centers on meeting ABC Company's nine learning objectives and building the best curriculum for the company's new hire sales training program.

Choosing a delivery methodology can be tricky. While one methodology has advantages that you feel are perfect for the learning situation, the disadvantages often weigh heavily against your first choice (see Table 7-1). When this happens, you might fall into the "if we could just" trap. For example,

- The self-paced design is great, but *if we could just* bring people together for two hours, we could be certain they are mastering the content.
- Participants love the classroom design, but *if we could just* reduce it from three days to two days in length without compromising the content, each delivery would cost $10,000 less.

Table 7-1. Advantages and Disadvantages of the Primary Training Delivery Methodologies

As discussed throughout this book, there are advantages (and disadvantages) to all of the primary training delivery methods: classroom, asynchronous, and synchronous. Here is a summary of these tradeoffs:

	Classroom	Asynchronous	Synchronous
Advantages	**Individual** Training happens in one spot and in a condensed timeframe Fewer disruptions because away from desk Familiar and comfortable environment Social aspect Physical aspect Immediate access to instructor **Facilitator** Training happens in one spot and in a condensed timeframe; once class is over the facilitator often has no more responsibility Tracking is easier Administratively less complex No need to learn technology to manage learning process	**Individual** Flexibility in scheduling Flexibility in location to take training Ability to review content **Facilitator** When a facilitator is used, flexibility in scheduling his or her time **Organization** Deployed enterprise-wide in a short period of time Easy to update content when necessary Easy to track course completion and assessments Consistency in message	**Individual** Flexibility in location to take training Learning is in shorter chunks—ability to practice or apply before moving on to next piece of content Social aspect: network building Access to a facilitator No travel Small class size **Facilitator** No travel Shorter class periods (but more frequent classes) Can develop stronger relationships with participants Small class size

	Classroom	Asynchronous	Synchronous
	Organization Training accomplished in a short period of time Short learning curve for instructors Easier tracking Administratively less complex Organization benefits of social networking among students Relatively easy to change content of curriculum when needed Able to allow for practice and application		**Organization** Travel not required Frequent offerings Shorter classes allow for more immediate application of skills More flexibility in topic choice (one- to two-hour courses are OK) Global reach—participants can be exposed to counterparts throughout the world Can reach individuals never reached before
Disadvantages	**Individual** Time consuming Takes away from regular duties Travel may be required Overwhelming amount of information—hard to practice before moving on to the next step No access to instructor once back on the job	**Individual** Need to be self-motivated to complete Limited or no access to an instructor Easy to be distracted Technology can be a barrier	**Individual** Easy to get distracted while at own desk Can feel disconnected from one's instructors and peers Technology can be a barrier Small group collaboration techniques need to be taught

(continued on page 152)

Table 7-1. Advantages and Disadvantages of the Primary Training Delivery Methodologies (continued)

	Classroom	Asynchronous	Synchronous
	Facilitator Travel may be required Difficult to ensure learning has taken place **Organization** Expensive: travel, classroom costs, time away from job Limited by number of facilitators and classrooms available	**Facilitator** When used, often required to support large "class size" **Organization** Depending on the technologies used: can be expensive to develop and maintain Best for knowledge-only objectives; hard to incorporate practice or practical application of skills	**Facilitator** Technology can be a barrier Hard to observe or assess mastery of an objective **Organization** (Perceived) takes longer to get through curriculum Investment in technology (both classroom and possible individual stations) Limited by number of facilitators available

DECIDING ON THE TRAINING DELIVERY METHOD

As training organizations mature and have access to more and more training technologies, they will often begin to experiment with mixing the delivery methods to solve business problems, such as reducing the amount of classroom expense (rent, meals, utilities), geographic separation, minimizing isolation during self-directed training, and just-in-time needs for training. Organizations must take note, however, of the ramifications of moving to a blended training delivery (see sidebar "10 Challenges When Creating a Blend").

As you may have noted in the previous chapters' examinations of the new hire training, each objective has different characteristics. Some objectives lend themselves better to activity-based training, while others tend to be more knowledge or lecture oriented. Going through the process of designing the best training approach on an objective-by-objective level allows for the exploration of a blended solution. While we are examining the objectives individually, we also must look at them in light of the whole curriculum to ensure that

---

10 Challenges When Creating a Blend

More than 60 individuals responded to a survey regarding the challenges they experienced when implementing a blended curriculum in their organization. Being aware of these common challenges will help you to manage them in your own design:

1. Ensuring participants can be successful using the technology.
2. Overcoming the idea that online learning cannot be as effective as classroom training (convincing stakeholders).
3. Keeping online offerings interactive rather than just "talking at" them (keeping the attention of the learners).
4. Ensuring participant commitment and follow-through during "non-live" elements (accountability).
5. Matching the best delivery medium to the objective(s)—arriving at the right blend.
6. Readjusting facilitator roles.
7. Looking at *how* to teach content—not *what* to teach.
8. Resisting the urge to use technology simply because it is available.
9. Ensuring all the elements of the blend are coordinated.
10. Managing and monitoring participant progress.

they are integrated, instead of each being its own independent learning piece that happens to be associated with the same topic (see sidebar "Beware the Blend 'Menu'"). In the blended design that follows, the order and execution of some of the objectives has changed to accommodate a more logical implementation of the training, given the overall business goal of helping new hires achieve success (and quota) by the end of their first six months.

For the blend to be most effective and to provide continuity for the participants, a workbook linking all the elements is crucial. The workbook should provide technical instructions, activity instructions, logistics, and contact information, as well as sales training content. Whether the trainee is participating in a discussion board, synchronous class, or self-paced tutorial, he or she will get all of their information from one printed, familiar source (see sidebar "PowerPoint Slides Are NOT the Same as a Participant Guide!").

Unfortunately, when most organizations move to a technological training orientation, they tend to view a workbook as "old-fashioned paper." In reality, it is imperative that participants have a reference guide that steps them through the learning process, gives them a place to take notes, and serves as a resource when they are back on the job.

CREATING THE BLEND AT ABC COMPANY

ABC Company has taken a thoughtful approach to updating their current curriculum by fully exploring all delivery options and using external experts to assist. The three individual designs presented in chapters 4, 5, and 6 each effectively address the objectives, are easy to implement, and are within the scope of ABC Company's training function capabilities. While each delivery

---

Beware the Blended "Menu"

As you will recall from chapter 1, a blended curriculum requires that all elements of the blend are integrated and often dependent on one another. Too often, however, organizations label something a "blend" when it is really a "menu."

Offering a "finance for non-financial managers" course in a one-day class, via a self-study e-learning download or by means of a three-session synchronous offering, does not constitute a blend. These are simply different options for the same offering; it is akin to the waitress at Denny's asking if you'd like fries, rice, or mashed potatoes with your meal.

PowerPoint Slides Are NOT the Same as a Participant Guide!

Don't fall into the trap of thinking you can send out a slide deck and call your participant guide done! Your participant guide should be more than a repeat of what is viewed on the screen—it should be the glue that holds the blend together. Technical notes, activity instructions, reading assignments, and key dates and deadlines should all be organized to help ensure participant success. Content needs to be included, of course, but organize the content in such a way that it complements what the participant sees on the screen—not just replicates it.

---

method is sufficient, blending them together can create a better solution from the perspective of learning outcomes, organizational implementation, and economic considerations.

Now that the program has been designed for the three delivery methods, the next step is to select the best method for each objective. Each approach, per objective, is reintroduced below, along with the approach that is deemed to be the best fit for ABC Company.

The opportunity to create a blend also gives permission to manipulate the timetable. Objective 7 (Closing a Sales Call) and Objective 8 (Managing Objections) will not be addressed right away. Instead, they will be dealt with when it is more appropriate to the participants' learning in terms of time and experience on the job. While this type of schedule was feasible in the asynchronous and synchronous stand-alone approaches, the momentum of the program may have been lost. A blended approach, combining self-directed work, live sessions, presentations to office colleagues, and other exercises, lends itself more to a continuum of learning and implementation rather than a program that has a definite start and end point.

Objective 1: Represent the Organization in a Professional Manner

In the classroom-based approach to this objective, the participants individually introduced themselves for five minutes throughout the course of the first day of training. Their fellow participants graded them, using a short checklist of presentation skills that included eye contact, body language, and vocal ability.

In the asynchronous approach, the participants learned about professionalism by reading their employee manual, which discussed dress and etiquette, and by watching a video of the president of ABC Company talk about the company's stature and reputation in the industry and stress the importance of the new hires to uphold that stature.

In the synchronous course, the participants also watched the video of the president and then had a brief, facilitated discussion about professionalism and what that looks and sounds like. Both the asynchronous and synchronous approaches attempted to assess the effectiveness of participants' professionalism in the context of a culminating presentation that the new hire was required to make to his or her field office at the end of the training period.

The Blended Approach. In the blended approach, the asynchronous design will remain at the beginning of the new hire training process, including the culminating presentation that the new hire must make to his or her field office at the end of the training period. Following are the two primary reasons for this approach:

1. While the classroom-based presentations were effective in giving people practice at presentation skills, they were done prior to actually learning any content. Inserting a different presentation requirement at the end of the training allows the participants to combine the knowledge and skills that they have acquired throughout the training into a more content-specific presentation.
2. There is no reason for participants to make presentations to fellow participants. The audience for the presentation is not as relevant as the presentation skills demonstrated by the participants themselves. The crucial factor is having a live audience that can offer feedback. Because of this, the asynchronous and synchronous approaches would not work as the best way to fulfill this objective.

Objective 2: Describe the Features and Benefits of the Company's Five Core Products to Prospective Buyers

In the classroom-based approach to this objective, the facilitator lectured on the five core products and the features and benefits of each, while the participants followed along in their workbooks. The asynchronous approach had the participants access an e-learning module, based in PowerPoint, which showed pictures and descriptions of each of the core products along with the product's features and benefits. The asynchronous approach was complemented by a workbook that included *all* of ABC Company's product offerings (30 in total), but highlighted only the features and benefits of the five core products. Participants were able to take notes about the products as they reviewed the PowerPoint presentation, and they also were instructed to gather marketing materials for each of the products to include in their workbook in association with the appropriate product.

The synchronous approach required the participants to first read through the product section of their workbook and come to class prepared to take a short quiz about the product offerings. After the quiz was debriefed, the facilitator presented a short lecture on the differences between features and benefits; then participants were divided into five groups, each assigned one core product. The small groups used a virtual breakout room to brainstorm the features and benefits of the product that they were assigned. A large group discussion followed.

The Blended Approach. The blended approach to this objective will include the asynchronous and synchronous approaches in their entirety. Participants will begin by utilizing a PowerPoint-based e-learning tool in conjunction with their workbooks, to learn about the 30 products that ABC Company sells. Subsequently, participants will come together in a synchronous (virtual) classroom to 1) take a quiz based solely on the five core products; 2) be taught new content regarding features and benefits led by the facilitator; and 3) participate in the corresponding breakout activity.

This approach was designed primarily for organizational and economic considerations. The e-learning content was retained because its use is not restricted to new hire salespeople; it can be an ongoing resource for all salespeople in the organization. In addition, the learning content is easy to update, should a product's features change or a new product be introduced. Finally, in conjunction with the mobile learning concept (see chapter 8), the e-learning can be utilized as an on-demand training or reference tool.

Objective 3: Compare and Contrast the Company's Core Products With the Products of Our Three Closest Competitors

The classroom design of this topic required participants to do a short independent exercise, researching ABC Company's top three competitors and their product offerings. Each individual was assigned one competitor and given 20 minutes to research that competitor's webpage. All participants assigned the same competitor then worked together to compare their findings and come up with a brief presentation for the rest of the class.

In the asynchronous approach, participants were given a research assignment also, but were required to research all three competitors using a job aid that helped them focus on the information they should be acquiring from the competitor's webpage. Upon researching each competitor, participants were instructed to use their workbooks to write a short synopsis of the competitor's offerings and how they compared with those of ABC Company. The synopsis was to be written in a way that the participants would eventually be able to use to describe the similarities and differences to a future prospect.

The synchronous approach started with the participants brainstorming their competition in the industry, critically thinking about who might be among their competitors. The brainstorming concluded with a short lecture by the facilitator, who zeroed in on the three main competitors and explained to the participants why those three were the closest competitors within the industry. The participants were then given time to do independent research on the Internet (while still in the synchronous classroom) on each of the competitors. Finally, they were paired with another participant and assigned one competitor and an ABC Company core product to compare and contrast with the competitor's offerings. The activity was conducted in a breakout room. After 20 minutes of pairs-work, the large group was reconvened and each pair was charged with giving a brief presentation about the competitor's offering.

The Blended Approach. This blend also will use a combination of the asynchronous and synchronous designs. Participants will begin this topic by using the job aid designed for the asynchronous learning to conduct independent research on each of the three main competitive organizations. Participants will then be assigned a partner to complete the same activity used in the synchronous design. This activity can be accomplished over the phone, because it is simply a conversation, or it can be done in a virtual breakout room. Finally, all participants will gather in a synchronous classroom where each pairs-team will give a presentation to the entire group about the one competitor and one core product they were assigned. An advantage of using the asynchronous assignment is that it allows participants all the time they need to conduct their research. This topic is one that would benefit from collaboration, however; so the synchronous design is also used to maximize learning and encourage reflection about each of the five core products and three main competitors. The pairs design was retained to ensure that every participant completed the assignment; if a larger group had been used, it would have been possible for an individual to opt out of participating, or to simply sit on the sidelines while others did the work. While collaboration is an essential learning process for this objective, there is no reason for the collaboration to be face-to-face; therefore, the synchronous classroom approach was retained.

Objective 4: Target High-Potential Prospects

The Profiling and Qualifying Tool was the basis for this objective regardless of the delivery methodology, even though each delivery method reviewed the tool by a different means. In the classroom, the review was a discussion led by the facilitator; in the asynchronous course, it was a narrated PowerPoint presentation describing the tool and its usage; and in the synchronous course, it was a discussion based on each participant interviewing their field office colleagues about the ideal prospect concept, followed by a demonstration of the tool by the facilitator. Regardless of method, once the tool was reviewed, the same activity was used for all delivery methodologies: Participants were given 10 sample profiles of potential clients and asked to rank them in terms of the best prospect to pursue, down to the worst prospect to pursue, based on using the Profiling and Qualifying Tool. The classroom and synchronous offerings concluded this objective with the facilitator debriefing the participant's work and correcting any errors. The asynchronous exercise concluded with the participants using the e-learning interface. They arranged the prospects in order from one to 10, with the system offering suggestions, and finally corrections, should the participants choose an incorrect order.

The Blended Approach. The blended design for this objective again includes a combination of the asynchronous and synchronous design approaches. Participants start by viewing the narrated PowerPoint presentation, then go on to ask questions of more senior salespeople in the office about the ideal characteristics of a prospect. Participants complete the rank-ordering activity using the 10 profiles; and finally, all participants meet in a synchronous classroom, which begins with a poll asking the participants to share their final prioritized list of prospects to pursue (see Figure 7-1). The facilitator will then conduct a discussion focusing on the reason the number one prospect earned that ranking, followed by a facilitated discussion for any rankings that appear to be controversial. This process will assist participants in articulating what they learned, including the information that they gathered from more senior salespeople, to better help them think through the rationale behind an acceptable prospect. This approach also will help the new hires become more familiar with the other salespeople in their office, which is an ancillary, beneficial outcome. The combined instructional approach is used because it is not necessary to have an instructor explain the ranking process; however, it *is* beneficial to collaborate to gain a broader perspective beyond the tool or beyond what one's peers in the office may think. Therefore the synchronous element is being kept to help solidify the learning for this objective.

Objective 5: Demonstrate the Ability to Open a Sales Call

All three designs employed the use of a commercially purchased video that showed various salespeople opening a sales call. The classroom and

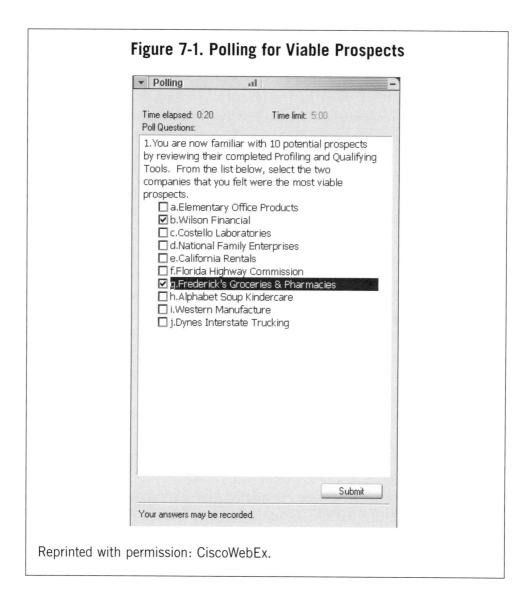

Figure 7-1. Polling for Viable Prospects

Reprinted with permission: CiscoWebEx.

synchronous offerings both utilized the facilitator to conduct a discussion after each vignette, focusing on the strategies or techniques used in the video. Each of these offerings also gave the participants time to practice opening a sales call by having them conduct role plays in triads with one participant playing the salesperson, another playing the prospect, and a third taking notes and offering observations. In the asynchronous offering, the facilitated discussion was approximated by a filmed facilitator offering a critique of the opening process. The asynchronous offering then required the participants to answer two to three questions about each vignette and post their responses in a common discussion board area to facilitate an ongoing conversation with their fellow participants.

The Blended Approach. The blended approach will utilize a synchronous approach: having participants watch the vignettes and the facilitator lead a discussion about each approach and its effectiveness. Participants will then accompany a senior salesperson on a number of prospect calls, as in the asynchronous design. Once participants have done their "ride-along," they will write a "diary entry" to the group discussion board, describing what they learned from their sales mentor. While opening a sales call is an important skill, and one that was practiced in both the classroom and synchronous approaches, the fact that they were role plays, and therefore contrived, really did not make them effective enough. Thus, practice will not occur at this point in the blend; rather it will be addressed during a capstone activity. (The capstone activity will be discussed later in this chapter.)

This combined approach is determined to be the most effective because, while it is beneficial to see how a sales call is opened, role plays can be too artificial. What better way to learn how to open a call than by observing a peer from one's office? A beneficial organizational outcome from this design may be that senior salespeople or mentors will constantly keep their own pipeline filled to have prospect calls at the ready when the new hire salesperson has reached that point in his or her curriculum.

Objective 6: Demonstrate the Ability to Manage a Prospect Meeting

The classroom and synchronous approaches to this topic both required participants to work in groups of three—in the classroom, they worked together in person; in the synchronous class, they worked together in a virtual breakout room—utilizing a completed Profiling and Qualifying Tool for a fictitious prospect. The groups were tasked with developing appropriate questions to gain more information about the prospect and his or her organization, and then suggesting an ABC product or service that would meet the needs of the prospect. In the asynchronous design, participants then reviewed completed Profiling and Qualifying Tools for two fictitious prospects and developed an appropriate set of questions to help clarify the prospects' needs, which they posted to the discussion board. The facilitators acted as the prospects and answered the questions, after which each participant determined the best solution(s) to meet those needs. These solutions, and their justifications, were posted to the discussion board for feedback from the facilitators and sales managers.

The Blended Approach. The blend will utilize an "un-facilitated" synchronous approach. First, each individual will complete a short off-the-shelf tutorial on how to ask effective questions that uncover the true need of the prospect. Then the entire group will be divided into teams of four, each of them assigned one completed profile for a fictitious prospect. The team will meet on the phone or in a virtual classroom to analyze the profile and send a list of questions to the facilitator via email. The facilitator will reply to any unique questions via email and, in addition, attach a prefabricated question-and-answer sheet that covers the five typical questions and their answers. The teams will then reconvene and choose one of the five core products to recommend. The group will make a short PowerPoint presentation to present at a synchronous class explaining the prospect profile, the questions they asked, and their recommendation and rationale (see Figure 7-2). Any other concerns or remarks will be discussed in an open forum during the synchronous session.

In the future, the participants will have to think of their questions in the moment while in discussion with a prospect, but during class, they will be given the opportunity to collaborate with colleagues to come up with the best discussion strategies. The collaborative activities, both in the small groups and in the large presentations or discussions, will help participants work in partnership with other salespeople as well as assist them in hearing different perspectives that will enhance their learning.

Objective 7: Demonstrate the Ability to Close a Sales Call

The classroom design and synchronous design each utilized video vignettes that demonstrated appropriate closing techniques. Following the video, a

---

Figure 7-2. Sample Slide Recommendation—Case Study

Prospect Profile: Urban School System

Product recommended: (fill in)

Questions you asked to lead you to product recommendation (at least five)

1

2

3

4

5

discussion with the facilitator allowed participants to first scrutinize appropriate phrases or methods to identify when a prospect is ready to close the sale, and then demonstrate closing the sale through the appropriate use of sales dialogue. Each design also included a final round of role plays, which allowed the participants to practice the entire sales process from opening the sales call, asking probing questions to identify need, and closing the sales call by using appropriate sales closing techniques.

The asynchronous approach to the objective also included the video vignettes with a filmed facilitator providing the associated debrief. The participant workbook included a job aid that detailed the steps of the sales process, from opening a call to closing the sale, and instructed participants to use it as a reference when on the job. The asynchronous approach lacked any practice time with the concepts.

The Blended Approach. With this objective, the blended approach takes off in a different direction. In the previous course designs, the process included opening a sales call, keeping the discussion going, closing the sales call, and then "what if" scenarios in the form of objections. The blended design recommends that the skill of closing a sales call not be taught right away; rather, it will be pushed off for eight weeks. There are three reasons for this postponement:

1. The practice role plays in the other designs forced a contrived practice of this skill.
2. We learned from the interviews in chapter 2 that no new hire salesperson will be ready to close a sale before the third or fourth month of employment. By the time participants are ready to close a sale, they very well may have forgotten everything they learned in the training class. By moving this objective further out, they will learn the skills when they have more chance of implementing them immediately back on the job.
3. Thanks to the blended design, there are no time constraints. Why not move the topic to a point in one's career when it would be more beneficial?

This approach allows the participants to use the Profiling and Qualifying Tool, identify prospects, go on their own sales calls, and practice keeping the conversation going—all before they learn the nuances of closing a sale.

Thanks to the use of training technologies, such as synchronous classrooms, this just-in-time approach to training is possible. Were the class to continue to be offered in the classroom, closing the sale would have to be taught within the prescribed training period, or the organization would have to fly people back for a second in-person meeting—and neither option is ideal in terms of achieving a learning outcome.

When the topic is addressed in the blended approach, the synchronous design will be used, keeping the video vignettes and discussion with the facilitator, and conducting role plays. However, the role plays will be handled a bit differently to keep everyone's attention. The entirety of the training group will be divided into groups of four. Each participant will have his or her own role-play situation and will meet in a synchronous session with three other trainees and the facilitator. The facilitator will play the prospective buyer in all cases. Each individual will get 15 minutes to practice the entire sales process with the facilitator (from opening the call, to continuing the conversation, to closing the sale), while the remaining participants take notes and offer feedback at the end of the role play.

Objective 8: Manage Objections

In the classroom design, the participants were divided into four teams and tasked with brainstorming various objections in a particular category, such as timing ("This is not the right time for us to make such a purchase") or budget ("It's not in our budget to replace equipment this year"). Each team then posed one of their objections to the three other teams, and those teams had to come up with an appropriate response to the objection. This parrying of objection and response continued until all teams had voiced all of their objections. The facilitators simply moderated the dialogue and corrected any mistakes or errors. The asynchronous design utilized an e-learning module that taught the basic types of objections and had participants play a game requiring them to categorize the objections they read on the screen. Once they had a basic understanding of the objections, they were instructed to poll the more senior salespeople in their offices for the toughest objections each individual had faced during their sales career; and then choose what they deemed to be the toughest objection to post to the discussion board for an asynchronous discussion with fellow trainees.

Objection gathering was an ongoing assignment throughout the first week of the synchronous design, and included asking the senior salespeople how they responded to the objection and whether the response was effective. Eventually, each trainee created a PowerPoint slide that included the toughest objections they had gathered, and passed that slide on to the facilitator, who categorized all submissions to build customized content for the discussion about objections in the live synchronous session. During the synchronous session, participants had the opportunity to respond to an objection and were critiqued by their fellow participants in regard to the effectiveness of the response.

The Blended Approach. Experience has determined that the skill of managing objections is best taught after the new hires have more practice at the organization. Therefore, the topic of managing objections will be addressed approximately six weeks after the new hire start date, because designers do not expect that participants will have to manage objections until they have been on the job for a few weeks. This topic will be taught in one two-hour synchronous session, which requires participants to first email the facilitator with objections they have encountered or problems they are coming across in terms of getting their sales practice up and running. The facilitator will then aggregate all submissions into one PowerPoint presentation, to maintain anonymity, and categorize them by the type of objection (money, authority, and timing). The synchronous session will be a facilitated, open discussion, run jointly by one facilitator and one sales manager. Ideally, the sales manager in attendance will be from an office that does not have a new hire in the training process at present.

The blended approach to managing objections introduces the topic at a more realistic point in the new hire's experience—on the job. By gathering objections and frustrations in advance of the synchronous meeting, both the facilitator and the sales manager have the opportunity to prepare appropriate examples and anecdotes. The most crucial consideration in regard to this objective is to get the six-week-out training date on everyone's calendars to ensure that it *will* happen and that all trainees will get the training associated with this topic.

Objective 9: Implement an Action Plan Designed to Meet Quota in the Specified Time Period

The goal setting and action planning topic was a major learning piece for each approach to the training. The classroom design had a guest speaker (sales manager) come to the class to discuss quotas, compensation, goal setting, and sales manager support. Then, given a template, each trainee was given time to create a plan of action to achieve his or her quota. The trainees also were given a follow-up assignment: to meet with their sales manager when they returned to their field office, so they could have a discussion about roles and expectations during their first six months on the job.

Because the asynchronous version of the training design had participants learning *from* their field office, the completion of the action plan and goal setting template was done in person, in conjunction with their sales manager.

The synchronous approach was very similar to the face-to-face approach, except participants were expected to meet with their sales managers immediately following the creation of their action plans and come to the final synchronous session prepared to compare and contrast the expectations of the various managers.

The Blended Approach. The blended approach to goal setting will combine both asynchronous and synchronous elements. First, participants will complete the goal setting template in conjunction with their sales manager. They will then attend a synchronous session to discuss, in an open forum, what expectations were set for them. The free-form discussion will allow participants to hear how different sales managers expect their new hires to get started successfully. The facilitator will help answer any questions participants may have about how to meet their managers' expectations or how to best utilize their manager as a support and future training tool.

The same synchronous session that addresses managing objections (six weeks into their employment) also will revisit each individual's action plan and manager expectations to determine whether the new hires are on track, or in need of additional assistance.

Capstone Activity

Blended curriculums bring with them legitimate concerns about a lack of continuity—moving from delivery method to delivery method can be disconcerting, and it can sometimes be difficult for a participant to mentally integrate all he or she has learned into a singular work process. In addition, some tasks and skills are better assessed in a face-to-face format. For example, Objective 1.4 (Utilizing effective body language and eye contact) is an interpersonal skill that requires practice in order to master; therefore, it will be addressed during a capstone activity. To ensure that the integration takes place, and to ensure that participants have the opportunity to apply what they have learned, each trainee will complete a capstone activity. This activity will take place approximately three weeks after the conclusion of the program. It will address all of the objectives with the exception of Objective 7 (Closing a Sales Call) and Objective 8 (Managing Objections).

Participants will schedule and make a presentation to their fellow, more experienced, salespeople in their field offices. The presentations will wrap up the presentation-oriented objectives, and will allow colleagues to quiz them on product knowledge and sales situations.

Participants will be responsible for creating and setting up the presentation and inviting colleagues to attend. The agenda should include

- a formal introduction of the new hire to the group
- three key takeaways from the new hire training program
- an overview of the five core products, delivered as if to a new prospect
- a question-and-answer period during which office colleagues can quiz the new hire on ABC Company's products, culture, and processes
- a wrap-up that includes the opportunity for colleagues to provide feedback to the new hire on professionalism, presentation style, and product knowledge.

Presentation attendees will complete an assessment that will provide advice on things like shaking hands, maintaining good posture, maintaining appropriate distance, and eye contact. Following the capstone activity, participants will have to write a short critique of their presentation and post that statement to the discussion board. They also will meet with their sales managers to privately review the presentation assessments, discuss areas of improvement, and determine if any additional training or practice opportunities are required. (If the answer is "yes," the participant will work with a training facilitator to set up the additional training.)

Linkages

The most crucial factor in the success of a blended learning curriculum is that all of the elements link to one another. You have noted that the blend includes a number of disparate training approaches. For instance, Objective 4 (Target High-Potential Prospects) starts with the participants using a self-study module on the characteristics of an ideal prospect for the ABC Company. Once the trainee has that basic understanding, he or she uses a tool to rank-order 10 potential prospects. Finally, the results of the rank-ordering exercise are brought to a synchronous learning session where the participants are able to compare their lists and discuss, with guidance from a facilitator, what the best deciding factors might be when choosing to pursue a prospect or not. The success of the virtual class discussion is dependent on the trainee completing his or her list; the completion of the list is dependent on an understanding of what constitutes an ideal prospect for the organization; and so on.

In addition, the objectives themselves are linked. One cannot overcome an objection (Objective 8) if one does not understand ABC's products in relation to the competition (Objective 3). Likewise, one cannot close a sale (Objective 7) without being able to successfully overcome objections (Objective 8). This purposeful linkage of objectives and activities within objectives ensures that no one (trainees, their managers, the facilitators, or the organization in general) views any part of the curriculum as "less important" than another. It circumvents the tendency to pick and choose certain elements of the curriculum or emphasize certain elements (in-person events, for example) over others (independent work and ride-alongs).

DELIVERABLE TO CLIENT—RECOMMENDATION

The final recommendation for a blend at ABC Company does not include a classroom training component. If participants were consistently co-located in one facility, blending some classroom time into the curriculum, perhaps in lieu of synchronous sessions, would be ideal. However, new hires could be located at any field office; so classroom training interspersed over several weeks does not make financial sense.

Weighing what needs to be done collaboratively against the costs and organizational factors that affect classroom training, we recommend that collaborative activities in the synchronous environment should be used, as long as guided practice opportunities are made available at the field offices. Table 7-2 outlines the recommended blended design.

Table 7-2. Recommended Blended Design

	Time Required	Asynchronous	Synchronous	Resources Required
Week 1				
Day 1		X		Video
1. Watch welcome video from president of ABC Company.	Three hours			VCR or DVD player
2. Read Section 6 of the employee handbook regarding dress code and appropriate office behavior; sign off on page 22 and fax copies to the HR department and training facilitator.				Employee handbook
				Fax machine
3. Read chapter 12 in *The Sales Bible* regarding rapport building.				*The Sales Bible*
4. Using PowerPoint presentation and a workbook, review the online learning module that covers ABC Company's core products.				Access to online learning module
5. Review the common client needs and ABC Company product alignment chart found in the workbook.				New hire training workbook
6. Meet with other new hires in synchronous session for review and quiz on ABC Company products.	60 minutes		X	

Day 2				
1. Use job aid to conduct competitor research (independent).	90 minutes	X		Job aid Workbook
2. Work with partner to analyze one competitor and one ABC Company core product; create presentation.	60 minutes		X	
3. Meet with other new hires in synchronous session for review and quiz on ABC Company products.	90 minutes		X	
Day 3				
1. Review characteristics of a viable prospect via online learning module.	60 minutes	X		Access to online learning module
2. Interview more senior salespeople regarding ideal characteristics of a prospect.	60 minutes			
3. Rank-order prospect profiles using workbook.	60 minutes	X		Workbook
4. Meet with other new hires in synchronous session for review and quiz on ABC Company products.	60 minutes		X	
Day 4				
1. In the virtual classroom session, watch a video on how to open a sales call.	Two hours		X	Video Workbook
2. Address discussion questions for each video vignette with facilitator and group.	Four to six hours			
3. Accompany senior salesperson from field office on prospect calls.				
4. Write reflective entry on discussion board following ride-along experience.	30 minutes	X		

(continued on page 170)

Table 7-2. Recommended Blended Design (continued)

	Time Required	Asynchronous	Synchronous	Resources Required
Day 5				
1. Independently complete tutorial on effective questioning techniques.	60 minutes	x		Tutorial
2. Working in teams of four, create a strategy to manage a fictional prospect, including appropriate questions to ask (this may be done over the phone or in a synchronous classroom).	Up to four hours	x	x	Worksheet PowerPoint
3. Share questions with facilitator(s) for feedback.			x	
4. Reconvene work group to choose one ABC product to recommend and create short PowerPoint presentation.	60 minutes		x	
5. Meet in synchronous classroom to make small group presentations regarding chosen prospect and recommendations.	Two hours			
Week 2				
One two-hour synchronous session will be held this week once all participants have met with their sales manager and set their sales goals with their manager. The session will be facilitated by a training facilitator and a sales manager, to help clarify expectations and provide guidance in achieving goals.				Workbook

This ends the formalized, daily learning process for the new hires. Additional learning modules will come in later weeks, as described here:

Week 6—Managing Objections. In advance of a two-hour synchronous session, the participants will email the facilitators a list of objections they have encountered while on the job during the first six weeks. The facilitator will categorize the objections from all participants. A synchronous session with all participants, one facilitator, and one sales manager will review the collected objections and provide insight into the probable reason for the objection, as well as potential ways to keep the conversation going with the prospect—rather than letting the objection put an end to the sales process. This session also will revisit sales goals and manager's expectations to assist the new hires in clarifying and achieving their sales goals.

Week 8—Closing the Sale. After eight weeks on the job, all new hires will meet in a synchronous session to watch five video vignettes representing various ways to close a sale. A facilitator will lead a discussion that points out various techniques and phrases. The entire group will then be divided into groups of four, and each foursome will meet individually, in a breakout room with the facilitator, to practice the entire sales process—opening the call, continuing the conversation, and closing the sale. Each individual will get 15 minutes of practice time, with the facilitator acting as the prospect, while the remaining three participants take notes and offer feedback after the role play has concluded.

THE TRAINING *AFTER* THE TRAINING

The blended learning solution addresses the primary objectives for the new hire sales training. A formalized two-week learning agenda with additional training opportunities over the first two months on the job will allow the new hires to learn at a reasonable pace, and efficiently apply what they have learned on the job.

However, this is just a starting point. ABC Company needs to provide more instruction on other topics to set new hire salespeople up for success. By creating a training structure that allows for development during the first six months on the job, the company can enable new salespeople to take advantage of resources that will help them be successful.

Each week through week 14 on the job will include a training opportunity. New hires will be provided with the schedule during their first week on the job, so conflicts can be minimized. Some training, like supplemental product training, will be required. Other training, like effective time management, will be optional but strongly recommended.

This "training after the training" continues the blend and creates a culture focused on employee success (see Table 7-3).

CONCLUSION

This chapter emphasized the importance of choosing the delivery method to support a learning objective. As you have learned in previous chapters, it *is* possible to achieve each objective in a variety of ways. But a truly blended curriculum chooses the best delivery method for the objective, considering learner needs (in this case new hires who should be welcomed and supported), the organizational environment (in this case geographically dispersed and working from a field office), and business goals (in this case anticipating a return on the training investment in the form of quality work performance and ultimately sales).

The next chapter examines leading-edge web collaboration technologies, including wikis, blogs, discussion boards, podcasts, mobile learning, and most recently, virtual worlds. Utilizing these collaborative technologies provides many benefits, from knowledge sharing and camaraderie across a distance to simple access to corporate history.

Table 7-3. Training *After* the Training Schedule

Weeks 1–6 (as time allows) Self-paced	Basic computer training How to use email, contact manager, shared calendars, MS Office products
Week 7 Eight hours of synchronous and self-paced content	Customer Relationship Management System training (required)
Week 8 Two-hour synchronous session supplemented by workbook with job aids and templates	Effective Time Management training
Week 9 Two-hour synchronous session	Use of mobile device (phone) to support field work (customer information, product specifications, general knowledge)
Weeks 10–11 Self-paced	Supplementary product training (product training on other than core products) (required)
Weeks 12–13 Synchronous kick-off session followed by asynchronous modules	What services do we sell to support our products, and how do we incorporate them into our sales presentations? How are we compensated for service contracts, and how does that relate to our six-month sales quota? (required)

Week 14 Synchronous session Supported by a wiki	Following through Don't be discouraged—a sales relationship takes time to build!
Week 16 Action plan update	A presentation by the new hire to the sales manager, detailing progress toward quota, and discussion of development needs (required)
Ongoing Coaching Every two weeks-plus, as needed	Each new hire will be assigned a coach, and will be required to have a lunch meeting every two weeks. This coach will be a true mentor, providing assistance and making recommendations to help the new hire in making quota. (required)
Ongoing Collaboration	Use of the blog, wiki, and discussion boards to increase knowledge and expand personal network; required postings for the first four months, optional thereafter (required)

Chapter 8

Collaboration Technologies
That Support Learning

N ow that the design team has determined the best blend, it might consider supplementing the training with some of the web collaboration technologies that are making headlines. Examples of web collaboration technologies include wikis, blogs, discussion boards, podcasts, mobile learning, and, most recently, virtual worlds (see sidebar "Definitions of Common Collaboration Technologies"). Synchronous and asynchronous learning, as commonly defined, support a formal learning process that has been tested and found to be effective. Web 2.0 technologies, however, are often used in less formal learning settings because of the opportunity to be more free-form and conversational in posting and responses.

The use of collaborative technologies can provide many benefits: knowledge sharing, camaraderie across a distance, a support network, and access to experts. Because much of the technology is relatively simple for a savvy Internet user to utilize, it has often been implemented with an "if we build it they will come" mentality, and sadly, many wikis and blogs are left unread and podcasts left unheard. This chapter explores the use of these alternative technologies in a purposeful way.

Definitions of Common Collaboration Technologies

Web 2.0: A term describing the trend in the use of World Wide Web technology and web design that aims to enhance creativity, information sharing, and, most notably, collaboration among users.

Blog: An abridgment of the term *web log;* a website, usually maintained by an individual, with regular entries of commentary, descriptions of events, or other material such as graphics or video.

Wiki: A collection of webpages designed to enable anyone who accesses it to contribute or modify content; often used to create collaborative websites and to power community websites.

Discussion Board: A web application for holding discussions and posting user-generated content; more linear in nature than a wiki.

Podcast: A series of digital media files distributed over the Internet using syndication feeds for playback on portable media players and computers.

Mobile Learning: Learning that happens across locations, or that takes advantage of learning opportunities offered by portable technologies.

Virtual Worlds: A computer-based simulation environment intended for its users to inhabit and interact via avatars; one of the widest uses of this technology is using 3D environments to allow virtual visits.

Source: Wikipedia, Wikipedia Definitions, The Premier Web 2.0 Collaboration Tool Defines Collaboration Tools. Retrieved June 10, 2008.

COMMON QUESTIONS

Before making a recommendation about whether or not to supplement the existing curriculum with Web 2.0 technologies, the design team needs to understand the "why's and how's" of the various technologies. Collaboration technologies can be effective, but they also can be viewed as "trendy" if not thoughtfully implemented. Designers who are considering including these technologies as part of their curriculum should think about the following questions (and their answers) as they pertain to their specific organization before investing time and money in these technologies.

Why Add a Blog or a Wiki?

Collaboration tools like blogs and wikis seem to be everywhere—but their purpose is not always apparent. A corporate collaboration tool needs to have more definition than "Go here to post or find information," and should exist to support the organization's goals. Later, this chapter will address specific implementation strategies for ABC Company, but, in general, the design team will recommend that blogs and wikis be implemented to serve the following purposes:

- Internal collaboration: to keep associates informed about new products, projects, or challenges in a centralized, easy-to-use location
- Knowledge management: to maintain a corporate history of facts, solutions, and other important information that would not normally be addressed in a more traditional training class.

Are All Web 2.0 Technologies About Collaboration?

It seems logical that collaboration tools are all about, well, collaboration. But, as the saying goes, "That ain't necessarily so!" While discussion boards and wikis encourage an ongoing group conversation, other technologies like blogs and podcasts tend to be oriented toward a subject matter expert, with the author positioned as a thought leader in the organization. Readers can post comments (either verbal or spoken), but the conversation, and therefore the level of collaboration, is directed by the designer.

Is Participation Required or Optional?

An established, functioning employee population will most likely resent time being eaten up by a "trendy" corporate requirement, and therefore, the rollout plan needs to encourage participation without being invasive. If participation is an option, providing employees with an incentive to contribute is a good idea. Start with a core group of advocates and sponsor contests for participation. For example, highlight contributors in a very public way on a periodic basis, and make sure that management is actively responding. An exception to optional participation might be new hires—requiring them to read company forums and post questions can help them get acclimated to the new organization.

What Kind of Moderation Is Required?

Unmoderated collaboration areas are dangerous places. Contributions could be incorrect, leading to misinformation being spread. Conversely, contributors' questions might go unanswered, resulting in the perception that the collaboration areas are not useful—a self-fulfilling prophecy. The key to collaboration

---

Choosing a Moderator

Web 2.0 technologies should be carefully monitored by someone who

- is truly interested in maintaining an open dialogue between contributors
- can create an environment that encourages collaboration
- has time to dedicate to moderation (several hours a week).

Consider using a moderation team of volunteers and lighten the load!

---

success is to have an advocate to insist upon the use of the tool, and to have someone responsible for maintaining it (see sidebar "Choosing a Moderator"). This person would be responsible for ensuring that posting guidelines are followed. Look for a volunteer from the training team or management.

COLLABORATION TECHNOLOGIES AT ABC COMPANY

So, what specific collaboration technologies should be implemented at ABC Company—blogs, wikis, or mobile learning? Let us explore the technological supports that are available.

What Are Blogs and Wikis?*

Inexpensive and easy to set up and manage, wikis, and especially blogs, have most often been viewed as vehicles for first-person online diaries or rants. Blogs and wikis are similar, with the major difference being the amount of control users are given. Simply, a blog allows one person (or others as designated) to post a thought or item, such as an image, link, or video clip, and optionally allows others to comment on that item (see sidebar "A Great Resource: Jane Bozarth's Blog" for an example). A wiki is more dynamic: Everyone with access can start discussions, change, add, or delete content and even pages.

There are many possibilities for the use of blogs and wikis as instructional tools. They offer a free or low-cost means of encouraging interaction and collaboration, and help engender a sense of community by reducing the "distance" between learners and between learner and instructor. In addition, they are simple for users to create, update, and manage, and can easily exist outside

---

*Thank you to Jane Bozarth of the Bozarthzone (http://www.bozarthzone.com), for her expertise in the area of wikis and blogs.

A Great Resource: Jane Bozarth's Blog

Jane Bozarth's blog is a great resource for training departments with limited budgets: http://bozarthzone.blogspot.com/.

bozarthzone

Notes from Jane Bozarth's Bozarthzone, with ideas for creating and outsourcing inexpensive e-learning solutions, along with general thoughts about the training and development field.

Reprinted with permission: Jane Bozarth.

---

the grip of the organization's IT department. Used as defined here, both blogs and wikis are simple means of creating class discussion sites, a place for inter-session assignments, and areas for student journals and updates from instructors (see sidebar "Sample 'Aha!' Blog Entry" for an example). Many free and hosted tools are available. For example, Blogger.com and PBWiki.com both offer free versions of their tools. More security can be added for professional (read: "fee-based") versions of the software.

In considering the instructional uses of these technologies, compare their capabilities with what is done in the traditional classroom to encourage collaboration, interaction, and community. Discussions, role plays, debates, written assignments, and projects come to mind, as do casual hallway, break, and lunch conversations. Blogs and wikis provide the perfect means for replicating many of these same activities, as do additional technologies such as

---

Sample "Aha!" Blog Entry

InSync Training's "Aha!" blog is actually a threaded discussion, which encourages participants to share their learning from each asynchronous module or live event that had the most impact.

Message #4 of 38

Subject:	Re[2]: a-ha! Blog
Posted:	Thursday, May 29, 2008 by Vickie Hadge 10:01 AM EDT
In Reply To:	Re: a-ha! Blog (posted by Kristin Packer)

My Aha! from this session is the power of the breakout rooms. They can be a very effective tool for collaboration. They do need to be used with lots of instruction for the participants though (verbal, participant guide, on screen) or they will be wooshed away and not know what to do.

I loved the shared exercises too. It is wonderful to see how others design their exercises; it gives me inspiration.

Reprinted with permission: InSync Training, LLC.

discussion forums and online communities. Discussion forums allow for threaded discussions (that is, several conversations can be going on simultaneously), and the nature of discussion forum software ensures that the discussions stay organized in sequence and by topic. These forums offer great opportunities for activities such as online role plays and debates (see sidebar "Don't Re-Create the Wheel").

How Can ABC Company Use Blogs and Wikis?

Implementation of these collaborative technologies is fairly easy

> **Don't Re-Create the Wheel**
>
> If an organization does not want to expend the effort to create its own collaborative knowledge centers, it can take advantage of commercially available resources. For example, "Sales Evolution" is a free "tips and techniques" blog for sales professionals sponsored by The Brooks Group (http://brooksgroup.com/blog/). At http://www.closingbigger.net/, salespeople can find a combination sales blog and podcast.

and inexpensive—the difficult part is the moderation. They do not maintain themselves, and rarely take on a life of their own. More often than not, they are started, then abandoned and discarded as just a fad. To reap the learning benefits of these tools, a moderator role needs to be established, and the responsibilities of the moderator spelled out. One strategy would be to have a different sales manager be responsible for presiding over the blog or wiki each month. Or, the sales trainers could alternate each month. To ensure participation, let salespeople know that their contributions to this "Continuous Learning Center" will be considered during annual performance reviews. The idea here is to kick-start the use of the asynchronous learning resources and create habits that eventually begin to self-perpetuate.

The most difficult part will be getting started. The sales managers and sales trainers will probably need to create an initial content base, so salespeople will have something to which to respond, and examples of what postings might look like. As the knowledge base grows, reviewing the history can become a required exercise for new hires and a great way for them to informally learn about ABC Company and its people.

These are some suggested forums for blogs and wikis:

- "Sales Trainer Tip of the Week": Each week, the sales trainer could post proactive advice to a blog, including topics such as these: "How would you have managed this objection?" or "Our competitor has a new product, and we don't have something comparable. Here are some suggestions for managing this conversation should it be arise." The blogs should attempt to anticipate questions, and arm the salesforce with critical information before they need it. As new advice is posted, text messages can be sent automatically to the salesforce. This "push" strategy ensures that everyone knows the information is out there.

- "Wiki Tips": Individual salespeople frequently have great tips and techniques to share, and new hires often don't have access to the wealth of information that more senior salespeople have accumulated based on their experiences. A wiki designed to capture best practices, "war stories," and other critical information (that would not be included in a formal training session) can be a great resource. New hires can post questions; more experienced people can answer; and then others can continue to comment and query. The wiki format allows the conversation to fragment in several directions, but allows the reader to follow any particular thread "upstream" to discover the genesis of the conversation.

- "Product Central": Product information is updated on a regular basis—but how is a salesperson to keep up? A blog for each product can keep everyone up-to-date. By reviewing the blog for products prior to each prospect call, a salesperson can be ready to answer just about any question.

WHAT IS MOBILE LEARNING?

Because of the ability to access collaborative training resources from almost any location, one of the latest trends in corporate training is mobile learning. According to M-Learning.org, mobile learning "is the exciting art of using mobile technologies to enhance the learning experience. Mobile phones, PDAs, Pocket PCs and the Internet can be blended to engage and motivate learners, any time and anywhere" (retrieved July 23, 2008).

Asynchronous e-learning provides curriculums *when* you need it. Synchronous learning provides curriculums *where* you need it. Mobile learning attempts to achieve both goals. After all, even the best e-learning tutorial on agricultural pest identification does you no good when you are in the middle of a field and have just discovered your crops have been decimated—the tutorial is no help if it is on the computer back at the farm, and the pest subject matter expert is 200 miles away. Mobile learning may be a way to solve your dilemma.

The incredibly successful June 2007 launch of the Apple iPhone is an example of the convergence of these technologies—consumers are becoming less willing to carry around multiple devices. As this convergence continues, the types and amount of instruction that will be delivered via mobile learning will surely explode.

Why Use Mobile Learning?

Educational institutions and businesses alike are seeing great advantages to using mobile learning. It is inexpensive to create, often depending on audio-only or text-only technologies. Because the use of graphics is minimal or nonexistent, bandwidth requirements are not high. And delivery technologies like audio-only podcasts don't require someone with a multimedia production background to create content.

Learning can occur when it is needed ("just in time") and, in theory, from wherever the learner happens to be. Sometimes, content is accessed from the local hard drive; other times it is accessed from the Internet—the idea is that mobile learning is ultimately convenient. Do you need to know how to fix a pressure gauge on an agricultural vehicle when you are 20 miles from the farm? Use your PDA to help guide you through the steps. Learning a new language? Listen to a podcast on your MP3 player, with headphones, while on the train to work. If you have an MP3 player with video capability, such as the Apple iPhone or iPod, you can observe a process, like the cleaning of a machine designed to shred cheese, and listen to the instructions as delivered by the narrator. If you need to review a step, it is easy to rewind and watch again. Museums and national parks (like the Minute Man National Historical Park in Massachusetts) are allowing visitors to use their mobile phones to access an audio-tour of their sites. Mobile learning is already all around us.

Designing Mobile Learning

The ease of use, low cost, and accessibility of mobile learning can lead practitioners into the trap of creating too much content with not enough thought about design. Those of us who recall early web-based training remember page-turners filled with useful content but lacking a systematic instructional design plan. Eventually, we learned that listening, reading, or watching four hours of content did not constitute learning. Content needed to be chunked by learning objective; learning needed to be assessed; learning styles needed to be considered; and learning needed to be active. Today's mobile learning designers need to incorporate these best practices to maximize the utility of mobile learning. When this is accomplished, mobile learning will become a ubiquitous delivery technology, providing access to content when and where it is needed.

How Can ABC Company Utilize Mobile Learning?

There are many ways ABC Company might use mobile learning:

- **As an on-the-job reinforcement tool.** Salespeople spend a lot of time traveling from place to place. To maximize this time, ABC Company can make a series of podcasts (recorded audio files) available. Content for these podcasts can include "Best Practices Dialogues" on topics like opening a sales call or introducing a new product line. Podcasts also can feature fellow salespeople sharing success or disaster stories. Many sales service providers offer commercially available sales podcasts. For example, the *SalesRoundUp* podcast (http://www.salesroundup .com), proclaiming to be the "#1 Sales Podcast in the World," provides a weekly video podcast with downloadable materials and a supporting blog. Topics offered include "Win the Negotiation Before It Starts!" and "It's Not What You Know It's Who You Know: Getting And Using Referrals."

- **As a quick response to prospect questions.** If a salesperson is on a sales call and is presented with a question he or she does not immediately have the answer for, the salesperson may ask experts within the company in "real-time," using instant messaging, or send an email to a help desk. Chances are an answer will arrive before the end of the meeting.

- **To access resources "just in time."** Prospects sometimes ask very technical questions, and it is almost impossible for someone to memorize, for example, the dimensions of every piece of equipment. Instead of saying "Let me get back to you," salespeople can use mobile technology, which allows them to say, "Let's look at that right now." Photographs, schematics, and product manuals can be accessed almost immediately, if the correct bookmarks are in place and the salesperson has been trained where to look.

- **To receive product updates and selling tips.** Small changes to a product can make a big difference to a salesperson, especially if he or she doesn't know what those changes are! Short updates with links to more detailed information can be provided on a regular basis via email or text message, and the salesperson can catch up while waiting for a plane or in between appointments. Salespeople do not need to remember every tip ever posted; this information can be archived on a website, potentially as a wiki or discussion board, so it can be accessed at any time. Relevant questions also can be posted and answered for the edification of all.

According to *Wikinomics* (Tapscott and Williams, 2008, p. ix), "The old notion that you have to attract, develop, and retain the best and brightest inside your corporate boundaries is becoming null. With the costs of collaboration falling precipitously, companies can increasingly source ideas, innovations, and uniquely qualified minds from a vast global pool of talent." Information collected and mined inside of the organization is at least as available as outside sources. Collaboration technologies are inexpensive and easy to use. To truly benefit the organization, mining the knowledge of ABC Company's salespeople, sales managers, and other experts will enhance the capabilities of the entire salesforce, not just new hires; and effective utilization can certainly help add to the competitive bottom line of any organization.

The design team recommends that only one technology be implemented at a time (a blog or podcast, for example), and success ensured before considering implementing another technology. Strategic, small successes over a period of time will help make collaboration a part of the culture, and not another fad. After a period of "enforced utilization," online collaboration will be recognized as a valuable resource.

CONCLUSION

This chapter offered some proven, but cutting-edge technology tools to add variety and just-in-time utility to ABC Company's blended learning solution for its new hire sales program. You should find plenty of ideas to incorporate in your own training solutions. The next chapter demonstrates the potential of blended learning from the perspective of four varied organizations through short case study scenarios. The four designs presented stand out because of both their simplicity and the benefit they provided to their respective organizations.

Chapter 9

Success Stories in Blended Learning

What follows are four case studies that illustrate the potential of blended learning no matter the industry or topic. This chapter provides blended learning curriculums, focused on a number of topical areas and offered to a variety of audiences, to assist the reader in seeing the variety of ways in which blended learning can be implemented. Of the 50 organizations that the authors polled about their blended learning curriculums, the following four designs stood out because of both their simplicity (using the resources and technologies already available within their organization and within their participants' capabilities) and the benefit their respective organizations derived from the blended curriculum. The examples include

- Case Study 1: Geographic diversity of participants (Continental United States, Pacific and Atlantic Islands) and limited number of trainers requires easily accessible training.
- Case Study 2: Public offering of a certification process that provides continuing education credits upon successful completion.
- Case Study 3: Trainees begin "real work" while still in training.
- Case Study 4: Flexible design allows each trainee to "customize" the training for his or her organization, *and* reduce the number of contact

hours from 20 to six, thereby allowing for a much lower break-even point for the organization.

BLENDED LEARNING IN ACTION

This book has addressed a very specific training topic, new hire sales training, from a number of delivery perspectives, culminating in a blended curriculum. Sometimes people have a hard time extrapolating from one example to their own situation. For example, what about a blended curriculum that addresses new hire training? Can a blend work in a government setting? The following case studies offer a variety of blended learning solutions, which tackle a number of different organizational and learning-oriented challenges.

Case Study 1. Globally Accessible Training

Case Study 1 examines how the Centers for Disease Control and Prevention, Division of Diabetes Translation (CDC/DDT), trains grant recipients and state agencies to use a web-based information system to capture data and generate reports. Because the participants are not required to participate in the training, the solution needed to be easy to access and of true value to the learner.

- Industry: Federal Government—Health Care
- Organization: Centers for Disease Control and Prevention, Division of Diabetes Translation, Atlanta, Georgia
- Curriculum designer: Mary Lowrey, Program Analyst
- Name of curriculum: Management Information Systems Training
- Training audience: Grant recipients—state agencies
- Time curriculum has been in place: Eight years
- Number of individuals who have completed the training program: 400 +
- Elements of the blend: Classroom, virtual classroom, telephone, printed reference materials, email
- Length of time it takes to complete the curriculum: Up to two weeks
- Mandatory or elective: Training not *required,* but necessary to do one's job
- Business goal or impetus for the blended curriculum: A new computer-based process to be rolled out across the Continental United States and its jurisdictions (Pacific Islands, Puerto Rico, Virgin Islands), combined with a limited number of trainers who possessed varying degrees of knowledge (therefore inconsistency in deliveries).

Synopsis. The Centers for Disease Control and Prevention collects data on various diseases from reporting agencies in the United States and its jurisdictions. In 1999, the way in which the CDC's Division of Diabetes Translation collected its data changed from a paper-based process to a web-based software process. This change required every reporting agency to learn a new web-based computer system and its reporting features.

The Design. To learn the software system in its entirety, participants need to complete five modules; each module is offered at least once per quarter. Three modules can be completed in one synchronous session, either classroom or virtual, while the remaining two modules are a combination of virtual classroom, asynchronous printed materials, and telephone support from the facilitator. A typical blended experience looks like this:

Participants from throughout the United States and its jurisdictions take part in an initial online meeting in a virtual classroom (LiveMeeting). The synchronous session is led by a facilitator who familiarizes participants with the course content and provides an overview of the software. Participants then go off to work independently on examples and projects, which are sent to them via email. If necessary, participants may confer with the facilitator via telephone while completing their asynchronous work. Participants reconvene for a follow-up session, via the virtual classroom, to discuss the work that they have completed and to answer any questions they may have developed as a result of doing the asynchronous work.

Because the DDT offers the training as a value-added service to its reporting agencies, and does not require attendance or completion, there is no formal assessment. However, the DDT has experienced a significant benefit from the training in the form of better data collection.

Lessons learned during the design or rollout of the blended learning curriculum:

- Network with other departments in your organization regarding available technology that is easily accessible to you.
- Allow for (schedule) time for yourself and the users to learn the technology you will be using *before* rolling out the curriculum.
- Do not cram all your lessons into a short amount of time; shorter segments and in-depth discussions are more effective for "genuine" learning.
- When something doesn't work, admit it, scrap it, and move on.
- Elicit feedback and ideas from your learners—and then act on their feedback.

Case Study 2. Corporate Training

Case Study 2 looks at an offering from a private consulting firm that certifies individuals to make the most of synchronous learning platforms (virtual classrooms) as instructional tools. The organization uses facilitators from throughout the world to conduct its training classes.

- Industry: Corporate Training
- Organization: InSync Training, LLC
- Curriculum designers: Jennifer Hofmann, SLE, and Nanette Miner, EdD, SLE
- Name of curriculum: Certified Synchronous Learning Expert (SLE)
- Training audience: Individuals who design or facilitate synchronous online learning; both public and private offerings of the certification are offered
- Time curriculum has been in place: Three years
- Number of individuals who have completed the training program: 75 people have become fully certified (completing all 16 weeks), while more than 600 have completed at least one element of the curriculum (facilitation or design)
- Elements of the blend: Synchronous e-learning, coaching, email, on-the-job learning assignments, asynchronous discussion board assignments, participant workbook, textbook
- Length of time it takes to complete the curriculum: 16 weeks for full certification
- Mandatory or elective: Elective (open to public enrollment)
- Business goal or impetus for the blended curriculum: Public demand for best practices in design and facilitation of synchronous learning offerings, from a recognized industry leader.

Synopsis. The Synchronous Learning Expert (SLE) certification includes three separate components: facilitation certificate, design certificate, and capstone certificate. Participants may choose to take either facilitation or design, if a single course fulfills their learning goals. If they choose to become a certified Synchronous Learning Expert, they must complete both certificates as well as a capstone certificate. All components have a required project component.

The Design. The facilitation certificate takes five weeks, with a final teach-back requirement; the design certificate takes seven weeks, with a one-hour synchronous course design project requirement; and the capstone certificate takes three weeks, and also includes a final course design project that demonstrates advanced skills (typically, a revision of the design final project and delivery of it).

While the courses differ in duration and topic, they are essentially designed in the same manner. Each course meets once a week for a two-hour, synchronous classroom session (if it is a public offering, WebEx is used; if it is an offering for a private client, the client may dictate that the virtual classroom platform to be used). There are inter-session assignments between each of the live, weekly sessions. Inter-session assignments consist of discussion board replies to questions that have been posted by a facilitator, textbook reading assignments, and on-the-job assignments, such as designing a collaborative exercise that utilizes the chat feature of a synchronous platform. The facilitator and a producer (assistant facilitator) communicate with participants via email during non-class days and also monitor the discussion board and answer any questions that may arise from the participants.

In the case of the design certificate, the producer also hosts a one-hour synchronous office hour during the week, which enables participants to receive just-in-time coaching and assistance while creating their weekly design assignments. Each certificate culminates in a performance-based assessment. The facilitation certificate requires a 30-minute teach-back before an audience of their peers. The design certificate requires participants to submit a minimum one-hour course design for the virtual classroom environment, including facilitator guide, participant guide, and supporting materials (typically slides, because all synchronous platforms use slides as their visual medium).

Lessons learned during the design or rollout of the blended learning curriculum:

- Every assignment or expectation must be thoroughly spelled out to ensure learner success (give examples, deadlines, and human support).
- Integration of the asynchronous and synchronous offerings is crucial, so that participants do not see one as "optimal" or "busy work."
- Establish a robust tracking system and ensure its usage.
- Detailed facilitator guides are necessary to make sure each offering is identical to the next (this is especially important when using contract facilitators).
- A producer (assistant facilitator) is critical both during the live sessions, to manage the technology, and "after hours" to stay on top of the asynchronous work (discussion board, submissions, feedback, coaching, attendance tracking).
- Allow enough time for the asynchronous work—both for the participants to complete the work and for the facilitator (or producer) to review any submissions.

- Use live class time for application and practice; use asynchronous time for purely knowledge-related pursuits like reading and discussion board postings.
- Constant communication with participants is crucial to ensure they feel connected to the class and don't drop out because "no one will notice if I'm gone."

Case Study 3. New Hire Training

Case Study 3 introduces us to a new hire training program for Arizona's Medicaid/SCHIP Agency. New hire training is a great way to introduce blended learning to the workforce. If they receive training online on Day 1 (or in this case, Day 2), they will understand that online and blended learning is the expectation for their organization. And because an increasing number of employees are hired to work from home, as well as in local field offices around the state, a virtual training solution makes even more sense.

- Industry: State Government—Health Care
- Organization: State of Arizona—Arizona Health Care Cost Containment System (AHCCCS)
- Curriculum designer: Rebecca Anderson, Training Manager, and the Division of Member Services—E-learning Design Team
- Name of curriculum: KidsCare New Hire Training
- Training audience: New hires to the AHCCCS/State Children's Health Insurance Program (SCHIP)
- Time curriculum has been in place: One year—four offerings
- Number of individuals who have completed the training program: 20 (sadly, the state instituted a hiring freeze shortly after the curriculum was rolled out)
- Elements of the blend: Asynchronous e-learning, virtual classroom, email or telephone, simulation, discussion board, on-the-job assignments, interaction with supervisor
- Length of time it takes to complete the curriculum: Nine days (the first two weeks of employment)
- Mandatory or elective: Mandatory (training represents the complete job skills training any new hire will receive)
- Business goal or impetus for the blended curriculum: Move a formerly classroom-based new hire training program to 100 percent virtual delivery.

Synopsis. Because the state agency is moving toward a virtual workplace, and to accommodate the employees in diverse geographical locations around the state, the training curriculum had to be moved from the traditional classroom to being delivered 100 percent virtually. One of the benefits of this new curriculum delivery was the ability of the agency to hire highly qualified individuals who lived nowhere near a physical location of the agency.

The Design. New hires go to their local agency location on the first day of employment to complete human resources requirements, meet with their supervisor, and meet with a trainer to get a sense of what the training will encompass. They take home-office equipment back to their homes and set up the equipment, so they can begin training the next day. Each day begins with a virtual classroom session (starting with LiveMeeting, then moving to iLinc), which gives participants the focus for the day, and ends with a synchronous session to answer any questions and review the material that they completed asynchronously throughout the day. The instructor is available via email or telephone throughout the day, while participants are completing their asynchronous assignments. At certain points in the curriculum, participants are required to email assignments to the instructor for feedback and coaching (which occurs via email or telephone). In addition, participants are required at various intervals throughout the course to post responses to discussion board questions. The discussion board entries tend to deal more with soft skills, while the assignments are computer-system oriented.

Once participants understand the process and the software used to correctly complete their job requirements, their supervisor gives them real work to complete while still in training. Because every individual is working on different cases (assignments from their supervisor), the facilitator must be highly skilled in both assisting individuals to complete their asynchronous assignments and facilitating the end-of-day discussions that are entirely dependent on the types of cases assigned by the supervisors. The final exam ensures that participants are able to complete the process and use the software correctly. The exam is the same exam that was formerly used in the classroom, but now it is delivered in a different format for the virtual employee.

Lessons learned during the design or rollout of the blended learning curriculum:

- Test all of the elements of your design before rollout.
- Don't expect or require everyone to be at the same place in the curriculum on any given day. Keep a general overview of what people should be accomplishing.
- Involve managers in the training process to build the relationship between the new hire and his or her supervisor.

- Create follow-up, reinforcement materials for the supervisors to ensure learning comprehension and policy adherence. Enable supervisors to access the e-learning modules later for use as a refresher or coaching tool.
- When moving classroom-based facilitators to online facilitator roles, make sure they understand the curriculum design and their role in the process (more of a facilitator or coach than an instructor).
- When possible, include real work rather than fabricated examples; this allows for faster transfer to the job.

Case Study 4. Flexible Curriculum Design

Case Study 4 looks at an in-depth, blended curriculum designed to support personnel responsible for highway maintenance and planning. A particular challenge existed because the curriculum had to be flexible enough to allow for state-by-state differences, while still using a common computer system.

- Industry: Federal Government—Public Safety
- Organization: Federal Highway Administration, National Highway Institute (NHI)
- Curriculum designer: Thomas Elliott, Training Program Manager
- Name of curriculum: Principles and Practices of Enhanced Maintenance Management Systems
- Training audience: State Departments of Transportation (DOTs); specifically the individuals involved in highway maintenance, from planning through evaluation
- Time curriculum has been in place: Two years
- Number of individuals who have completed the training program: Six
- Elements of the blend: Asynchronous e-learning (PowerPoint), virtual classroom, printed workbook, on-the-job assignments
- Length of time it takes to complete the curriculum: 16 hours, in the course of one week
- Mandatory or elective: Elective
- Business goal or impetus for the blended curriculum: The NHI needed to become more efficient in its use of funding because of its widespread customer base (all 50 states) and the relatively few number of people who require this training in any particular state (five to seven individuals). In addition, while more states and municipal entities (large cities, for example) have begun to request the training, the number of people requiring the training has decreased, making a minimal course enrollment increasingly difficult to achieve.

Synopsis. This training curriculum had historically been offered as a classroom-based course, which required participants to travel to a central location and was held only when 20 to 30 participants were signed up. Participants were charged for the training and, because of the high costs of classroom-based training, a minimum of 20 participants was necessary to cover the expenses of a room, facilitator, and materials for a two-and-a-half-day course. To better utilize its resources and serve its market, which was expanding to private industry and large cities, the NHI sought an alternative way to offer the training. This course was the pilot course in anticipation of migrating many NHI training offerings to a blended design, which could take advantage of asynchronous resources and synchronous technologies.

The Design. There are eight lessons included in the curriculum, followed by a culminating exam:

Monday: Lessons 1 and 2 are conducted via a two-hour virtual classroom (Adobe Breeze—Connect) session. Lesson 1 is simply an introduction to the course; Lesson 2 is an introduction to maintenance management systems. This first synchronous session includes small group activities in virtual breakout rooms.

Tuesday: Lessons 3 and 4 are completed asynchronously using the maintenance management systems in place at each individual's organization (state).

Wednesday: A second synchronous session is offered—also two hours. During this session the facilitator reviews Lesson 1 content, and participants review the work that they completed independently. An open discussion, with questions and answers, is facilitated by the instructor.

Thursday: Lessons 5, 6, 7, and 8 are conducted asynchronously. Participants access the lesson materials online. Lessons 5 through 7 cover data requirements, integrating the maintenance system with other systems, and a maintenance management system implementation plan—again, all specific to the individual participants. Lesson 8 is a review lesson that highlights the key concepts from all lessons and prepares participants for the final exam.

Friday: The final synchronous session is also two hours. The facilitator reviews the key points from Lessons 5 through 8, the participants report back on their independent work activities, and an open question-and-answer period is facilitated by the instructor to ensure that participants are clear on expectations and learning. The final exam is an online evaluation of 20 questions based on the learning outcomes.

Lessons learned during the design or rollout of the blended learning curriculum:

- Although the participants were widespread (from Virginia to Montana), discussion among them, about policies and practices within their own state agencies, was helpful in understanding the material.
- A workbook is crucial to guiding the learning for the participants, especially in assisting them to complete their asynchronous assignments. Initially, a workbook was not part of the design; however, because of participant requests, it was added before the end of the first rollout.
- Chat, in the virtual classroom, is important for two reasons: 1) It allows for participants to further their learning by discussing concepts with one another; and 2) it enables the facilitator to judge how effectively the participants are following the content and altering their approach, if necessary.
- The participants appreciated the ability to access the learning materials at their own pace and the ability to immediately use what they learned on the job.

CONCLUSION

The four case studies offered in this chapter illustrate very different approaches to blending learning curriculums and demonstrate that a successful approach does not need to be technologically complex or expensive. Rather, an effective blend needs to meet the needs of the participant and the organization, as well as accomplish the learning objectives. Start with a simple design and make a good impression—that will make it much easier for the organization to accept the next blended solution.

The next and final chapter offers a look at the future of blending learning solutions.

Chapter 10

The Impact of Blended Learning

"**T**here's never time to do it right, but always time to do it over." A sad axiom, but, when it comes to training curriculum design, one that applies to too many situations. In the case of blended learning, mistakes in implementation are often the cause of making decisions based solely on technology rather than on creating a well-designed program. For example, if an organization has a synchronous classroom, then often that is the delivery option that they utilize, without thought to appropriateness with regard to learning objectives.

ABC Company, our case study client, invested time up front to conduct a detailed analysis of its design options, so the chance of having a successful implementation is high. It won't be perfect—continuous evaluation of the training results will need to be conducted and the design will need to be tweaked. However, the technologies used are not complex and require no specific expertise; therefore, making small adjustments should not be too difficult.

Because ABC Company went through the process of considering four distinct options (redesigned classroom experience, asynchronous, synchronous, and blended), it should be relatively easy to implement changes to the design if the needs of the business change—factors like market demand, economic forecasts, or changes to hiring procedures—because options have already been considered.

Looking back to the design recommendations allows the designers to quickly recall what was considered and why each decision was made. And if any particular objective needs to be totally redesigned, that redesign can be accomplished in a vacuum, without a disruptive impact on the rest of the design.

WHAT IS NEXT FOR ABC COMPANY?

Any change requires a change in management strategy, and this includes the re-engineering of a training curriculum. Even if the design works as planned, ABC Company has some work to do. Following are some of the items that need to be addressed in the change management plan.

Impact on Design. This is the first cohesive blended learning initiative implemented at ABC Company. Tools need to be purchased, learned, and supported to develop the content and track completion. The design needs to be integrated to the point where it does not seem like many small programs, but rather one overarching curriculum.

Impact on Facilitation Team. This blended learning design presents a huge shift for the facilitation team—truly moving from "sage on the stage" to "guide on the side." The facilitators need to learn how to use technologies, and, more important, effectively facilitate and communicate within those technologies. What was once a two-day program has now been extended to almost three months, and more, if you consider the "training *after the training.*" This extension will change the nature of the facilitator-participant relationship. Also, the two facilitators will be more of a team, rather than independent lecturers. This experience has the potential to be very stressful for all involved, and ABC Company will need to strive to support the team by providing training, rehearsal time, and the ability to get extra assistance as needed as they go through the change process.

Impact on the Organization. Rolling out a blended learning solution for the new hire sales training curriculum will take much longer than the familiar two-day training program. However, it will provide the participants with many more opportunities to practice what they have learned, and to build new skills upon existing skills. If embraced, the effectiveness of the new hire salespeople should go up. Therefore, after the growing pains have subsided, ABC Company should have a much more competent salesforce—not only the newly hired, but also their longer-term counterparts—as successive groups complete the training.

A side benefit to the organization is the opportunity to test out a blended solution, and determine if a similar approach should be considered for other curriculums.

Impact on the Job. New hires, and their sales office colleagues, need to invest in the concept that learning at one's desk is a worthwhile use of time. That time needs to be respected by colleagues and supported by the sales manager.

Once the learning routine has been established, participants will benefit from learning within their true work environments. No questions need be theoretical, and the application of knowledge can be applied quickly to real work situations.

Assessment Plan. ABC Company should be able to determine fairly quickly if the investment in blended learning is working by comparing the percentage of salespeople who make quota after the blended learning curriculum to the percentage of salespeople who previously made quota (on average). Other metrics that can be compared include

- Percentage of salespeople who exceeded quota and by how much
- Satisfaction of participants with the training
- Satisfaction of sales managers with performance of new hires.

WHAT IS NEXT FOR BLENDED LEARNING?

As blended learning becomes more commonplace, the processes for implementing a blend will become more streamlined. Organizations will start to realize more returns than just those that come from any individual successful curriculum. Organizations will have employees who are more productive because they are able to learn the right content at the right time in the most appropriate format. The ability to learn in blended environments will naturally lead to the ability to work in blended environments, leading to the use of tools like virtual classrooms and wikis beyond the classroom and into the worldwide workplace.

The migration from stand-alone learning to a true blended format will not be easy—training teams and training audiences will need to adopt new tools and learn to communicate in different ways. Trainers accustomed to delivering content in a live, face-to-face format will need to adapt to facilitating asynchronous interactions as well as live interactions online. Participants conditioned to live, onsite instruction will need to take more responsibility for their own learning by completing self-directed work, actively participating in asynchronous activities, and being fully present during remote training situations.

Where are we going to be in 10 years? Probably living and breathing blended learning. We will wonder what all the fuss was about. We will realize that blended learning is so natural that we have been learning that way all along—the difference is we now have myriad new technology-based options to deliver content. The key is to match the learning objective to the most appropriate delivery medium. As designers start to master creating the blend, participants, facilitators, and organizations will have the benefit of the blend that truly fits.

References

American Society for Training and Development. *2007 ASTD State of the Industry Report.* Alexandria, VA: ASTD, 2007.

Bonk, Curtis J., and Charles R. Graham, eds. *The Handbook of Blended Learning: Global Perspectives, Local Designs.* San Francisco: Pfeiffer, 2006.

Gitomer, Jeffrey. *The Sales Bible: The Ultimate Sales Resource.* New York: HarperCollins, 2008.

Marx, Raymond J., and Karen Hudson-Samuels. *The ASTD Media Selection Tool for Workplace Learning.* Alexandria, VA: ASTD, 1999.

Rossett, Allison. *The ASTD E-Learning Handbook: Best Practices, Strategies and Case Studies for an Emerging Field.* New York: McGraw-Hill Professional Publishing, 2002.

For Further Reading

Bozarth, Jane. *From Analysis to Evaluation, with CD-ROM: Tools, Tips, and Techniques for Trainers.* San Francisco: Pfeiffer, 2008.

Clark, Ruth, and Richard Mayer. *e-Learning and the Science of Instruction.* San Francisco: Jossey-Bass/Pfeiffer, 2003.

Driscoll, Margaret, and Saul Carliner. *Advanced Web-Based Training Strategies.* San Francisco: Pfeiffer, 2005.

Edmundson, Andrea, ed. *Globalized E-Learning Cultural Challenges.* Hershey, PA: IGI Global, 2006.

Hofmann, Jennifer. *How to Design for the Live Online Classroom: Creating Great Interactive and Collaborative Training Using Web Conferencing.* Sunnyvale, TX: Brandon Hall, 2005.

———. *Live and Online!: Tips, Techniques, and Ready-to-Use Activities for the Virtual Classroom.* San Francisco: Pfeiffer, 2004.

———. *The Synchronous Trainer's Survival Guide: Facilitating Successful Live and Online Courses, Meetings, and Events.* San Francisco: Pfeiffer, 2003.

Kruse, Kevin, and Jason Keil. *Technology-Based Training: The Art and Science of Design, Development, and Delivery.* San Francisco: Pfeiffer, 2000.

Mantyla, Karen. *Interactive Distance Learning Exercises that Really Work!* Alexandria, VA: ASTD, 1999.

Rosenberg, Marc. *Beyond E-Learning.* San Francisco: Pfeiffer, 2006.

Shank, Patty, ed. *The Online Learning Idea Book.* San Francisco: Pfeiffer, 2007.

About the Authors

Jennifer Hofmann is a synchronous learning expert and the president of InSync Training, LLC, a consulting firm that specializes in the design and delivery of synchronous e-learning. In the e-learning field since 1997, she has experience using all of the major web-based synchronous delivery platforms. Hofmann holds a master of education degree from Nova Southeastern University, with a concentration in instructional technology and distance education. For years, the synchronous training community has had an abundance of tools, but a dearth of best practices in facilitation and instructional design. Hofmann's company has closed this gap with the synchronous learning expert (SLE) curriculum, which includes 35 hours of web-based synchronous instruction, blended with intensive self-directed work and rigorous individual projects. The unique, experiential approach allows participants using any synchronous platform to develop their synchronous learning.

Nanette Miner, EdD, has been an instructional designer for two decades. She is the founder and chief consultant for The Training Doctor, LLC (www .trainingdr.com), founded in 1991. The Training Doctor specializes in work-ing with subject matter experts to take the knowledge from their heads and design learning in such a way that others can adopt and implement their skills immediately. Miner is unique in that she is able to design curriculum for all delivery mediums including the traditional classroom, asynchronous and syn-chronous e-learning, or a blend of all mediums. A popular speaker at industry conferences for more than a decade, Miner is the author of *The Accidental Trainer* (Pfeiffer, 2006). Miner also edited *How to Design for the Live Online Classroom: Creating Great Interactive and Collaborative Training Using Web Conferencing* (Brandon Hall, 2005) and founded the nonprofit organization

The Accidental Trainer, which is a community of and support group for people who have found themselves thrust into the role of training from other lines of business.

Index

In this index, *f* represents a figure and *t* represents a table.

A

ABC Company
    asynchronous learning at, 87–89
    blended solution for, 154–55
    change management plan for, 196–97
    deliverable for, 167–68, 168*t*–71*t*, 172*t*–73*t*
    description of, 16–17
    mobile learning at, 183
    needs analysis for, 17–28
    questions for, 39, 41, 47
    redesign of, 55–56, 58, 78, 79*t*–81*t*, 82*t*–83*t*, 195–96
    web collaboration technologies at, 178–81, 184
    See also organizations
action plan objectives
    asynchronous, 109–10, 109*t*
    blended, 165–66
    classroom-based, 76–78, 77*t*
    synchronous, 138–39, 138*t*
activities, capstone, 166–67
agendas. *See* schedules
AHCCCS (Arizona Health Care Cost Containment System), 190–92

analyses
    audience, 18–19
    design, 30–31
    environmental, 19–21
    learning objectives, 9
    materials, 39–40
    training, 37, 41, 42*t*–47*t*, 48*t*–51*t*
    See also data collection; evaluation; needs analysis
Apple iPhone, 181
Arizona Health Care Cost Containment System (AHCCCS), 190–92
assessments, 22, 57, 61, 100
assignments, pre-work, 58–59, 59*t*, 61
ASTD E-learning Handbook, 4
ASTD Selection Tool for Workplace Learning, The, 87
ASTD State of the Industry Report, 33–34
asynchronous learning
    at ABC Company, 87–89
    action plans in, 109–10, 109*t*
    advantages/disadvantages of, 6, 10*t*–12*t*, 86–87, 150*t*–52*t*
    competition in, 96–97, 96*t*, 99
    definition of, 5, 85–86, 86*f*
    development time for, 87
    facilitators in, 88–89
    objections in, 107–9, 107*t*